Churches in America

Churches in America

By Thomas Manteufel
Edited by Arnold E. Schmidt

CONCORDIA PUBLISHING HOUSE · SAINT LOUIS

Copyright © 1994 Concordia Publishing House
3558 S. Jefferson Ave., St. Louis, MO 63118-3968
1-800-325-3040 • www.cph.org

The quotations from Lutheran Confession in the publication are from the BOOK OF CONCORD: THE CONFESSIONS OF THE EVANGELICAL LUTHERAN CHURCH, edited by Theodore G. Tappert, copyright © 1959 Fortress Press. Used by permission of Augsburg Fortress.

Unless otherwise stated, Scripture quotations are taken from the HOLY BIBLE, NEW INTERNATIONAL VERSION®. Copyright © 1973, 1978, 1984 by International Bible Society. Used by permission of Zondervan Publishing House. All rights reserved.

The "NIV" and "New International Version" trademarks are registered in the United States Patent and Trademark Office by the International Bible Society. Use of either trademark requires the permission of the International Bible Society.

09   10   11   12   13   14   15   16   17   24   23   22   21   20   19   18   17   16

Contents

Introduction

You are about to take part in an overview and discussion of the beliefs of religious denominations in the United States and Canada. This course is limited to Christian denominations or denominations often viewed as being Christian. You will have the opportunity to grow in your understanding of the many voices in the world speaking about Christ.

Perhaps you are not very familiar with your neighbors' churches and convictions and would like to know more about them. Or perhaps you are acquainted with them—at least to some extent—and would like help in evaluating them. This course will serve you in both ways. It will also help you appreciate your own church's teachings as you compare them with others in the light of God's Word.

This guide serves as a resource for private study, for participants in group study, and for study-group leaders. "Helps for the Leader," statistics for the church bodies mentioned in this book, and a bibliography follow chapter 8. Helps for answering the questions also appear here, except for the questions that call for personal reflection or opinion.

Prepare for each session by reading the chapter and working through the questions. Feel free to ask additional questions about the subject and its implications or to contribute to the discussion in other ways.

You and the other members of your group will probably have observations, experiences, and opinions to share from your contacts with other churches or thoughts about the points of doctrine involved. As this happens, you and they have a fine opportunity to support one another's faith and to help one another deal with spiritual difficulties and conflicts. Let a prayer for the edifying light and power of God's Word in each session be a part of your regular preparations.

All Bible quotations are taken from the New International Version. Other translations can, of course, also be used for comparison and clarification.

References to passages in the Lutheran Confessions include indication of page numbers in the Book of Concord as translated and edited by T. G. Tappert. The book is listed in the bibliography.

1

The Christian Approach to the Study of Denominations

What do Episcopalians teach? What is the difference between the Baptists and the Disciples of Christ, if any? Does it matter if I join the Presbyterian Church or the Methodist Church, or the Roman Catholic Church? What is a World Wider? Should I marry a Quaker? Why are there so many church bodies, if Jesus Christ set up only one church? If I go to a church body that just calls itself by the name Christian, isn't that the simplest, least troublesome way to arrange my religious life? Or do they all teach more or less the same thing anyway?

These are some of the questions often heard in America as people encounter the numerous religious groups. The 1992 *Yearbook of American and Canadian Churches* listed 216 bodies that are part of visible Christianity in the United States, not including Jews and other non-Christians, or groups for which the yearbook did not have statistics. For many this is a bewildering variety of organizations, forms of worship, and patterns of life. Some people are acquainted only with the beliefs of their denomination; others have had no religious training at all; and still others have played denominational "hopscotch," moving from church to church to church. This situation is complicated by the fact that many church members have little or no understanding of just what their denomination teaches.

Throughout church history controversies have existed involving differences of teaching between religious groups. These have arisen from sincere, though often fierce and angry, disagreements over points of Christian teaching and practice. A typical example is the story of the two ministers arguing over the positions of their respective denominations. At last, one said that they had the same Lord but that each worshiped Him in his own way. The other replied, "You worship Him in your way—and I in His way."

This brings up a question that must be asked in the midst of all the conflict of teaching in Christendom: Is there indeed an approach to doctrine and life that can be called "His way," that ought to be followed, and that can be identified by a norm to be applied? This question will receive a yes in the pages of this book.

Why We Should Deplore Divisions

Christians everywhere deplore the divisions that have torn visible Christendom apart. They remember the biblical truth that all who have saving faith in Jesus Christ are one body (1 Cor. 10:17). They are aware of the difficulty in reconciling the disruption of the churches with what the apostle says in Eph. 4:4–6:

> There is one body and one Spirit—just as you were called to one hope when you were called—one Lord, one faith, one baptism; one God and Father of all, who is over all and through all and in all.

What a glaring contrast occurs when groups come into being because of selfish ambition and conceit (Phil. 2:3)! Or when a spirit of factionalism shows itself in the forms of ungrounded claims or magnifying of personalities—like the spirit Paul attacked in Corinth:

> One of you says, "I follow Paul"; another, "I follow Apollos"; another, "I follow Cephas";

still another, "I follow Christ." Is Christ divided? Was Paul crucified for you? (1 Cor. 1:12–13)

Many Christians have reasons to be confident that their separation from others who profess Christ is an act of faithfulness to Christ and His Word. Even such Christians can still acknowledge with sorrow that the act can be done in an unchristian way. The faithfulness often includes unfaithfulness to admonitions of Scripture such as "Love one another" (John 13:34); and "The acts of the sinful nature are obvious: ... hatred, discord, jealousy, fits of rage, selfish ambition, dissensions, factions and envy" (Gal. 5:19–21).

Tragically, the disunion of professing Christendom creates difficulty for the non-Christian world whom Christian missionaries (and their Lord) are trying to reach. Those outside Christianity are understandably confused by the chaos of groups and repelled by the disgrace of it. Many are discouraged from joining the church. Which of the many churches should they join?

The problem for missions is not merely the disunity of competing organizations. Even if all presently existing denominations would be fused into one organization that is broad enough to include all their differences of belief, non-Christians would still find a great disunity of beliefs and teachings in this superchurch. Such disunity would confuse and offend them. We need a united church presenting a united message of grace and truth to the unbelieving world.

Denominational divisions are deplorable in many ways. Above all, many errors and departures from revealed truth have been inherited and perpetuated by such divisions. Those errors have often caused controversies within the various groups. There is disunity about many questions: What authority does Holy Scripture have? Should we rely on good works for salvation? Does Baptism have saving power? Is Jesus Christ our divine Substitute for sin? These and many other conflicts are deeply distressing to the soul who longs to hear the truth taught in the Christian church.

Holy Scripture treats erring teachings as a serious problem. We find solemn warnings against being carried away by false doctrines (Heb. 13:9; Eph. 4:14). Clearly, the Lord does not wish that such error be taught among His people, for He says: "Let the one who has My word speak it faithfully" (Jer. 23:28).

Scripture presents a beautiful picture of the church life the Lord desires to exist on earth. His people use the truth of His Word for mutual enlightenment and support. St. Paul writes,

> Each of us should please his neighbor for his good to build him up.... For everything that was written in the past was written to teach us, so that through endurance and the encouragement of the Scriptures we might have hope.... I myself am convinced, my brothers, that you yourselves are full of goodness, complete in knowledge and competent to instruct one another. I have written you boldly on some points, as if to remind you of them again. (Rom. 15:2, 4, 14–15)

God desires that Christian teaching be used for building up one another (Eph. 4:29; 1 Thess. 4:18; 5:11). We can be glad and thankful for all the occasions when it does take place, also sometimes between Christians of different church bodies. But frequently the leaders and members of religious bodies fail to agree on how to understand and apply the Word of God. This interferes with the Lord's design for mutual edification.

The Teaching Task of the Church of Christ

The church of Jesus Christ is composed of all those who believe in Him as their divine Savior on the basis of the Gospel. It is "all those everywhere who call on the name of our Lord Jesus Christ" (1 Cor. 1:2). This describes the body of Christ, the one holy Christian church mentioned in the Nicene Creed.

The Savior founded His church on the scriptural foundation of the proclamations of prophets and apostles (Eph. 2:20). Accordingly, He sent it out with this commission:

"Go and make disciples of all nations, baptizing them in the name of the Father and of the Son and of the Holy Spirit, and teaching them to obey everything I have commanded you." (Matt. 28:19–20)

God directs the leaders and people of His church to teach the whole truth of God faithfully and to guard and warn against departures from it.

We are to have a love for whatever belongs to sound doctrine and its expression in a Christian life and a hatred for whatever jeopardizes that. So, for example, we find St. Paul denouncing the errorists in Gal. 1:8–9 and those who denied the resurrection in 1 Corinthians 15. See also Titus 1:9–11 and 2 Cor. 11:13–14 for expression of this theme.

The Lord desires that His church continue steadfastly in His Word (John 8:31–32) and be careful about doctrine. He compared false doctrine to yeast.

"Be careful," Jesus said to them. "Be on your guard against the yeast of the Pharisees and Sadducees." ... They understood that He was not telling them to guard against the yeast used in bread, but against the teaching of the Pharisees and Sadducees. (Matt. 16:5, 12)

The church is right to fear that erring doctrine will spread and become more and more damaging. Paul explains, "A little yeast works through the whole batch of dough" (Gal. 5:9).

Not only the pastors and teachers, but all the members of the church have the obligation and privilege of professing, defending, and using the truths of their faith. Paul exhorts the Thessalonian Christians, "So then, brothers, stand firm and hold to the teachings we passed on to you" (2 Thess. 2:15).

All believers should be growing in right knowledge of their Savior and of sincere repentance and the Christian life of obedience. Pastors have the awesome responsibility of leading and strengthening their people in this and helping them avoid spiritual harm. This is the aim of the Lutheran church. Its Confessions state that it explains the Word of God

so that well-meaning Christians who are really concerned about the truth may know how to guard and protect themselves against the errors and corruptions that have invaded our midst. (Formula of Concord, Tappert edition, p. 503)

The Church and the Churches

As already stated, the one holy Christian church is made up of all who trust in Jesus as Savior. We call this the invisible church, since we cannot look into other people's hearts to see if they have faith. The visible church is made up of all those who profess the Christian faith. It contains some who profess without truly believing. The visible church is organized into many bodies or denominations. These differ in many ways in teaching and practice, often mixing truth and error. But all these bodies are known as "churches," for the sake of the one holy church that does exist in each one. The Lutheran theologian C. F. W. Walther put it this way:

> The name "church," and, in a certain sense, true church, also belongs to those visible companies of men who have united under the confession of a falsified faith, and therefore have incurred the guilt of a partial departure from the truth, provided that they possess so much of God's Word and the holy sacraments in purity that children of God may thereby be born. (Thesis 3 of the Altenburg Debate)

But some religious bodies insist that they be called Christian even though they deny central Christian doctrines, such as the Trinity and the divine/human reality of Christ. In this book we will refer to such groups as *cults*. These include the Unitarian-Universalists, the Mormons, and the Jehovah's Witnesses.

A religious group that organizes as a visible form of the church of Christ should commit itself thoroughly to what it believes. It will do the confessing, teaching work of the church as described above. Acts 2:42 says the early believers, "devoted themselves to the apostles' teaching." This characteristic of the church is often called "the confessional principle." Usually a church will adopt statements or creeds to explain their beliefs and will see to it that these beliefs are taught.

The Church in Ancient Times

Jesus sent out the leaders of the church with the command to preach repentance and remission of sins in His name among all nations. He said, "You will be My witnesses in Jerusalem, and in all Judea and Samaria, and to the ends of the earth" (Acts 1:8).

Disagreements in the Church

Throughout the history of Christianity, church leaders have attempted to carry out the church's responsibility of confessing and teaching the Word. At times they have differed in their conceptions of how to understand and express the Christian message. This has often led to controversies and formations of separated groups.

Even in the earliest days of the church some groups advocated deviant teachings that they claimed were the true doctrines of Christianity. Some examples:

The Judaizers in the first century. They taught that Christians must be circumcised and keep the Old Testament ceremonial laws to obtain salvation.

The Gnostics in the second century. They taught that the Creator was a different God from the Father of Jesus and that Jesus did not have a true human body.

The followers of Arius in the fourth century. They denied the deity of Christ.

The Macedonians in the fourth century. They followed Macedonius in calling the Holy Spirit a creature.

The Pelagians in the fifth century (followers of Pelagius). They denied original sin.

The of Nestorius in the fifth century. They denied that the divine nature and the human nature of Christ use each other's attributes or characteristics.

The followers of Eutyches in the fifth century. They taught that Christ had only a divine nature.

Defending the Faith: The Creeds

Rather than unite with any of these groups, faithful Christians contended against them to defend the revealed truths of Scripture that were involved, namely:

There is but one God, who has created heaven and earth.

The first human beings brought sin into the world by their disobedience, and their descendants inherit a deep corruption in which they are unable to deliver themselves from damnation.

The Creator in His boundless love for sinners has sent His Son, true God and true man, into the world to redeem them and restore them to fellowship with Himself.

God the Holy Spirit creates in human beings the faith that trusts in Christ as Savior and brings them into the fellowship of the church.

The church treasures and teaches these and other truths. It has summarized them in statements of belief and committed itself and its teachers to these statements. The best-known are the Apostles' Creed, the Nicene Creed, and the Athanasian Creed. These are commonly called ecumenical (worldwide) or catholic (universal) creeds, meaning they express the faith held by the Christian church throughout the world.

The Apostles' Creed affirms teachings of the apostles, teachings the church used to strengthen believers and to guard them against errors about the Father of our Lord Jesus Christ, and the like.

The Nicene Creed emphasizes the deity of Christ and the Holy Spirit. It originated at the church's Council of Nicea, which opposed Arius.

The Athanasian Creed was traditionally (but inaccurately) ascribed to Athanasius, the famous opponent of Arius. It beautifully teaches the doctrines of the Trinity and the person of Christ. It rejects the false teachings of Nestorius and Eutyches.

The Church Divides between East and West

A large and tragic division, known as the Great Schism, came about in 1054. Along with political and cultural factors, doctrinal differences led to a split between Western Christianity and the Eastern Church (Eastern Orthodoxy). For instance, the Eastern Church refused (and still refuses) to teach that the Holy Spirit proceeds from both the Father and the Son.

Over the years many erroneous teachings and corrupt practices arose. Numerous groups came into existence, promoting both right and wrong opinions. These include the Albigenses, the Waldeneses (who followed Peter Waldo), the Hussites (followers of John Huss), and the Lollards (followers of John Wycliffe).

The Bishop of Rome claimed to be the divinely appointed head of Christ's church, and believers have an obligation to recognize him as such. This became a major distinguishing doctrine of the Roman Catholic Church. The Bishop of Rome was to be called the *Papa* (Latin for "Father") of the whole church. From this come the terms *papacy* and *pope*. The papacy was (and is) regarded as a necessary provision from God for obtaining salvation through works of atonement and merit by God and man.

The Church in the Modern Period

Key events in the reformation of the church took place in Germany when Martin Luther attacked the church's false doctrines about salvation. On Oct. 31, 1517, he nailed the famous 95 Theses to the door of the Castle Church in Wittenberg. Luther's theses challenged the indulgences issued and sold by the pope to cancel punishment for sin. Luther warned against having false confidence in indulgences and against the authority of the pope. This hinders true repentance—heartfelt sorrow over sin and seeking grace and forgiveness in Christ and the Gospel—Luther said.

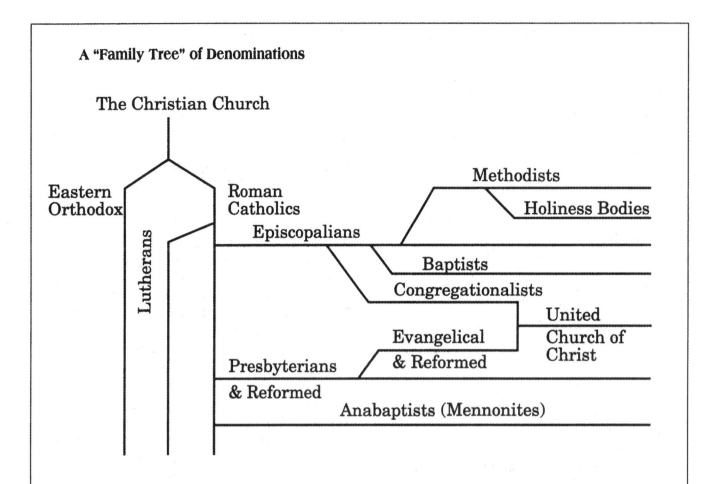

A "Family Tree" of Denominations

The Christian Church

Eastern Orthodox

Roman Catholics

Lutherans

Episcopalians

Methodists

Holiness Bodies

Baptists

Congregationalists

Evangelical & Reformed

United Church of Christ

Presbyterians & Reformed

Anabaptists (Mennonites)

This simplified chart shows denominational groups that have resulted from the divisions of the Reformation. It can be consulted in connection with the following chapters. Most bodies today can be described as branches on this "tree." However, the chart does not show groups that have arisen independently, such as the Quakers, Disciples of Christ, Seventh-Day Adventists, Jehovah's Witnesses, Mormons, Christian Scientists, and Unitarians.

A controversy was set ablaze by the publishing of the 95 Theses. Luther was compelled to search the Scriptures to obtain a thorough grounding of the teaching of justification through faith and related doctrines. He soon came to have a clear understanding that sinners cannot rely at all on their own good works, or on their attempts to pay for their sins, or on the pope, but solely on Christ as their Substitute and Savior. He affirmed that he found his guiding light in Rom. 1:17: "The righteous will live by faith." Sinners gain righteousness and peace through faith in Christ. This is the central teaching of the Lutheran church.

Various other groups also opposed the Church of Rome, but disagreed with Luther in various doctrines of the Christian faith. The followers of John Calvin in Switzerland, southern Germany, France, and the British Isles have become the Reformed and Presbyterian churches. The Mennonites and related groups advocated extreme change. The Church of England followed Calvinism and other influences. Other groups—such as the Congregationalists, the Baptists, the Quakers, and the Methodists—arose in England over time. Statements of doctrine came into being as all these explained their beliefs.

The churches of the Old World were brought to the New World by colonists and immigrants. In an atmosphere of religious freedom they developed in various ways and formed splinter groups. Also, a number of new religious bodies were founded in America, such as the Disciples of Christ, the Pentecostals, the Seventh Day Adventists, the Jehovah's Witnesses, the Mormons, the Christian Scientists, and the Spiritualists. In addition, innumerable cults are being added in modern times.

The Christian at the Whirlpool

This course is a study of the religious groups in America and an examination of their teachings in the light of the Word of God. Its purpose is to give teachers of our church a general acquaintance with the whirlpool of religions they see all around them and help them give some guidance to their students, who stand at the edge of that whirlpool.

What should be the attitude with which we approach this study? As a child of God, your attitude will be shaped along the following lines.

You will, first of all, desire to be faithful to the Word of God, through which you have received a knowledge of Christ the Savior. Scripture is the source of the pure doctrine of Christianity and the indispensable standard by which we judge all teachers and doctrines. Blessed are the children who learn to know and use the Scriptures as God's holy Word.

False doctrine in the church is not only an aberration that displeases the Lord, but an evil containing dangers to faith and to one's relationship to Him. Often it interferes with the assurance of salvation and with knowing God as He wants to be known by us. No better preparation for life (and coming to the whirlpool of religions) can be given than to lead a child to joyfully use God's Word.

It is natural that you take an interest in how other believers express their faith. This refers, of course, to those who do express it. We have noted that a lot of church members do not know or may not care what their denomination teaches. But many do have definite views and make use of instruction and reflection. These people are making use, in one way or another, of the doctrinal heritage of their church body. They are often aided and guided by teachers that have influence among them.

When we try to find out what people believe, we should avoid a spirit of prideful belittling or loveless contention. Rather, we should have a sincere desire to know one's neighbors better and to be able to speak with them about matters important to them. Occasions may arise to agree heartily with them when they state a truth about God and the Christian life. Occasions may also arise to warn against some danger we see in their belief.

As you learn to know what your neighbors believe, you are likely to make different kinds of discoveries.

You may often find points of agreement, where the traditions you honor say the same thing. You can rejoice together about this as fellow Christians and talk profitably about the biblical basis for the common beliefs and hopes.

You may find individuals that agree with you that their doctrinal heritage is wrong in some teachings. Again, you can strengthen each other from God's Word.

You may find some who disagree with a point in their own tradition that you recognize as truly Christian. You can use the opportunity to urge them to reconsider and return to the truth, an approach described by Dr. Hermann Sasse, an Australian Lutheran. He pleaded with a Roman Catholic friend to have faith in the resurrection of Christ on the basis of the Word: "Father, you believe that. You have believed all your life. You will believe it again. But there is a superhuman power that tries to destroy your faith."

You may become convinced that friends are being led astray by some parts of their tradition. You can warn them against the danger.

You may find a case of the old Swedish saying: "A man may be better than his doctrine." That is, he may state harmful errors about Christ or grace or the Gospel—statements that conflict with saving faith. But he believes otherwise; he *does* have saving faith. In theology this is called "the happy inconsistency."

You may find that the heritage that molds your neighbor's thinking is so perverted that it cannot be recognized as truly Christian. It and they have lost the trinitarian Gospel. Again, you have an opportunity to witness.

The chapters of this book present significant beliefs and practices of the American churches, including some groups that are "churches" only in the loose sense mentioned above.

The doctrinal heritage of each is described, bearing in mind that the members of a group may modify or depart from that heritage. Major doctrinal statements of heritage are identified, as is the extent of the commitment that each group requires of its members.

The church bodies of America may seem to form a large and bewildering variety of organizations, beliefs, and practices. But these can be grouped into a handful of families, or categories, which appear in the next seven chapters. Within these categories the relationships between the religious bodies can be studied conveniently.

Only selected bodies will be mentioned by name in the following pages. You will, of course, know or hear of others—for example, different kinds of Baptists, or Methodists, or Lutherans. They may have some points of teaching in common with more than one of the families. They may have some "family quarrels" in doctrine with groups to which they are related and similar. In any case, this course will give you some ideas for thinking and talking about groups that are not mentioned in this course.

> ### The Lutheran Vantage Point
>
> *In this course we examine denominations from a Lutheran point of view. But we always attempt to describe their systems of teaching fairly.*
>
> *When the beliefs of these non-Lutheran systems disagree with Scripture, we shall point out why such teachings cannot be considered acceptable.*
>
> *On the other hand, we shall note with pleasure those teachings that emphasize beliefs also found in the Lutheran Confessions. those teachings often make applications to Christian life, etc., from which Lutherans can gladly learn.*

Something to Think About

1. Why do you think there are so many church denominations today?

2. Mention reasons for deploring divisions in Christendom. Is there ever a time when division is necessary? Explain.

3. Explain the teaching task of the church. How does this glorify God and benefit human beings?

4. Does it really matter to which church you belong? If so, why?

5. Select one teaching of your church and explain how, in a practical and meaningful way, it affects your everyday life.

6. What is the distinction between "the church" (as referred to in the creeds) and "the churches"? How are they related to each other?

7. Discuss the question in the fourth paragraph (page 9) of this chapter.

8. Suppose someone says to you, "I don't know what to believe about God or whether it makes any difference what I believe. What is your belief?" Give a brief answer.

9. Find the Apostles' Creed (*Lutheran Worship—LW*—pp. 142–43; *The Lutheran Hymnal—TLH*—p. 12), the Nicene Creed (*LW*, pp. 141–42; *TLH*, p. 22), and the Athanasian Creed (*LW*, pp. 134–35; *TLH*, p. 53). Why do they have these names? Why are they called the *ecumenical* creeds? Make a list of the biblical teachings found in them.

10. What false doctrines are mentioned in this chapter as troubling the early church? Find statements in the three creeds that express Christian teaching that could be used in combatting them. If you wish, select one of the doctrines about which there was a controversy, do some research about it, and report to your group during a later session.

11. Name some groups that originated in the Old World. Name some groups that had their origin in America.

12. Explain this sentence (from the section "The Church in Ancient Times"), "The papacy was (and is) regarded as a necessary provision from God for obtaining salvation through works of atonement and merit by God and man."

13. What is the meaning of the saying quoted in this chapter, "A man may be better than his doctrine."

14. List the kinds of discoveries you might make as you talk with people who are members of other church bodies. If you wish, share some experiences you have had.

15. Look at the Table of Contents for this book. What observations do you have about the categories used to classify the religious bodies?

16. What do you hope to gain from this study?

2

The Lutheran Church

During the early 1500s, Dr. Martin Luther corrected many articles of the Christian faith that had long been obscured and corrupted by human doctrines and traditions. As a result, the Lutheran church came into being.

Luther and his followers maintained that they were preaching doctrines that had a history reaching back to the Scriptures of the prophets and apostles. They and their churches have commonly been called *evangelical,* which is derived from the Greek word for "Gospel." The name emphasizes their belief in justification by grace through faith, apart from works.

Lutherans throughout the world form the largest church that has resulted from the Reformation and, in the United States, the third largest. Immigrants from Germany and Scandinavia to the United States formed many

The Beginning of the Reformation

On October 31, 1517, Martin Luther nailed his 95 theses on indulgences to the Castle Church door in Wittenberg, Germany. In them he called for Christians to live a life of sincere repentance and of faith in Christ.

He urged reliance on the merits of Christ rather than on the indulgences issued by the church. He protested the idea that the indulgences released sinners from punishment after death.

As Luther searched Scripture in the controversy raised by posting these theses, God led him to understand that we are justified through faith alone.

groups, which have gone through a process of mergers. The two largest groups today are The Lutheran Church—Missouri Synod (LCMS), organized in 1847, and the Evangelical Lutheran Church in America (ELCA), formed by merger in 1988. The LCMS remains a separate body because of objections to ELCA's tendency to allow doctrinal freedom.

Statements of the Lutheran Heritage

The Lutheran Confessions contain the Lutheran heritage of doctrine. These are also called *symbols,* meaning "marks of identification." The Lutheran Symbols identify Lutherans by stating what Lutherans believe and confess. They set forth the answer to the question: "What does the Lutheran church teach?"

The Lutheran Symbols are called *confessions* because Lutherans have used them from the beginning to confess the doctrines of their faith. Those doctrines are drawn from Scripture; often the confessions use the very words of Scripture to express doctrine. But Christians also need to be able to use other, nonbiblical words to express the same doctrines and communicate them to others. The church needs summaries of biblical doctrine and refutations of false explanations of the message of salvation.

In time certain outstanding statements of faith became prominent and officially approved among Lutherans. These do not supplant or supplement the Scriptures. Rather the confessions proclaim the content of Scripture.

The Ecumenical Creeds

Critics accused the Lutherans of departing from the faith held by the Christian church from the beginning and of introducing new, strange doctrines. To answer this, the Lutherans declared their wholehearted acceptance of the ecumenical creeds. The ancient church had used these creeds to confess the faith and to reject false doctrine. These are the Apostles' Creed, the Nicene Creed, and the Athanasian Creed.

The Augsburg Confession

The followers of Luther were accused of introducing false doctrines and failing to observe ceremonies necessary for salvation. Charles V, Emperor of the Holy Roman Empire, called a Diet (or princes' assembly) in Augsburg in 1530. At this Diet the Lutheran rulers submitted a confession of the faith preached in their territories. Luther's co-worker, Philip Melanchthon, wrote the Augsburg Confession. It began with a quotation of Ps. 119:46: "I will also speak of Thy testimonies before kings and shall not be put to shame" (Tappert, p. 23).

Articles 1–21 set forth the doctrines taught by Lutherans on the basis of the Scriptures. Articles 22–28 give the reasons why Lutherans abandoned the sacrifice of the mass, compulsory celibacy, and other traditions that conflicted with Gospel teaching.

The Augsburg Confession is the foremost confession of the Lutheran Reformation. It has been the major badge of identification for Lutherans throughout the years. It is sometimes known by its Latin name, *Augustana.*

The Apology of the Augsburg Confession

At the Diet of Augsburg the Roman Catholic theologians attacked the Augsburg Confession in a book known as the *Confutation.* The Emperor claimed that the Confutation proved from Scripture that the teachings of the Augsburg Confession were false.

Melanchthon wrote a defense, or apology, of the Augsburg Confession and enlarged it after the diet. Published in 1531, the Apology of Augsburg Confession presents in more detail the scriptural grounding of the Lutheran teachings, above all the doctrine of justification by grace through faith.

The Smalcald Articles

In 1536 Luther drafted a statement of basic agreements and differences between Lutherans and Roman Catholics for use in case a general church council should be held the next year. (It was not.) These articles were adopted during a meeting of Lutherans in the city of Smalcald in 1537.

At the time of this meeting Melanchthon wrote a document called *Treatise on the Power and Primacy of the Pope.* The Lutherans regarded this as an appendix to the Smalcald Articles (Formula of Concord, Solid Declaration X 21; Tappert, p. 614). It is also a supplement to the Augsburg Confession.

Luther's Small and Large Catechisms

The two catechisms are actually the earliest of the Lutheran Confessions, written in 1529. They were written for the instruction of laypeople. The Small Catechism was a short handbook of questions and answers. The Large Catechism provided an explanation in greater detail. They are called "the layman's Bible" (Formula of Concord; Tappert, p. 465) because they express the essence of Scripture in a simple and appealing way. They cover the Ten Commandments, the Apostles' Creed, the Lord's Prayer, and the Sacraments.

The Formula of Concord

After Luther died, heated controversies arose among Lutherans about original sin, conversion, justification, sanctification, the Lord's Supper, and other matters. Concord (or agreement) on the basis of scriptural teaching was brought about by the use of a statement of faith titled the *Formula of Concord,* completed in 1577. It restated traditional Lutheran teaching.

The Formula of Concord called for unanimous approval of all the confessions that have been mentioned. All of these were published in a single volume on the 50th anniversary of the Augsburg Confession in 1580. This is called the *Book of Concord.*

The Confessional Principle

These famous statements of the Lutheran heritage are not only used for communication and education. They also serve as rule and standard for judging the acceptability of preaching and teaching in the Lutheran church. Lutherans do not regard the Confessions as a second norm added to the norm of Scripture. Rather, they hold that the Confessions are in full agreement with Scripture and therefore are nothing more than the application of the norm of "Scripture alone."

Therefore all Lutheran pastors and congregations are asked to pledge their loyalty to the Symbols. The Lutheran Confessions themselves call for Lutherans to accept them because they agree with Scripture in all teachings. This leaves no room for the option of accepting them only *insofar as* they agree with Scripture. The Lutheran pastor, in his ordination vow, is expected to be convinced that the Lutheran Confessions are in accord with Scripture and to reject the errors they reject.

Source of Doctrine

The sole source and standard of teaching in the Lutheran church is Holy Scripture. It is given by inspiration of God and is God's Word in all its parts, in order to make us "wise for salvation" (2 Tim. 3:15). It is infallible and reliable in all that it says. As Luther said, "God's Word cannot err" (Large Catechism, IV 57; Tappert, p. 444).

All Scripture bears witness to the Gospel of salvation in Jesus Christ. God speaks through the writers concerning the entire historical framework of the Gospel, its relation to the Law and all doctrines, and its diverse connections with the circumstances of life.

God's Word serves as the basis for the church's teaching.

> The Word of God shall establish articles of faith, and no one else, not even an angel. (Smalcald Articles, II II 15; Tappert, p. 295)

> We believe, teach, and confess that the prophetic and apostolic writings of the Old and New Testaments are the only rule and norm according to which all doctrines and teachers alike must be appraised and judged, as it is written in Ps. 119:105. "Thy Word is a lamp to my feet and a light to my path." (Formula of Concord, I 1; Tappert, p. 464)

Doctrines of the Lutheran Church

Following is a summary of several key doctrines of the Lutheran Church.

God

The one true God is three persons, Father, Son, and Holy Spirit, equal in power and majesty, and each possessing the entire divine essence. This doctrine has been revealed to us as the basis of our justification.

Apart from the Word of God human beings can come to know God only as Maker and Judge, strict and angry over sin. But the Bible teaches that each person of the divine Trinity plays a role in the sinner's salvation. We therefore recognize the Father's attitude of love, the Son's redemptive work, and the Spirit's justifying grace (2 Cor. 13:14; Matt. 28:19; John 1:1, 14; 3:16; 1 Cor. 2:7–14; 6:11).

Man

Man, along with everything else in heaven and earth, has been brought into being by God, in the way revealed in Scripture. The first human beings were created in the image of God, in true knowledge of Him and perfect righteousness and holiness. By the fall into sin they and all their descendants lost their original righteousness and are by nature dead in sin and under divine wrath. They cannot by any efforts of their own reestablish right relations with God; they need divine grace for reconciliation (Gen. 1:27; Rom. 5:12; Eph. 2:1–3; 4:24).

The Savior

Jesus Christ is true God, begotten as the Son of God from eternity, and also true man, taking on human nature in the womb of the Virgin Mary. As man He became the perfect substitute for sinful human beings, and as God He provided an infinite and all-sufficient atonement for every one of them. He satisfied the demands of God's Law by keeping its commandments in our place. He bore the punishment for our disobedience by His holy suffering and death. He rose bodily from the dead, ascended into heaven to reign over all things at the right hand of the Father, and shall come again to be the Judge of the living and the dead (1 Tim. 2:5–6; 1 John 5:20; 1 Peter 3:18–22; Acts 17:31).

Justification

God does not accept people on the basis of their own works but justifies them by grace alone, on account of the merits of Christ. That is, He declares as righteous those who believe that they are forgiven and acceptable to Him for the sake of His beloved Son. Since God has sent His Son to be the Savior, faith in Christ is the only means by which we may obtain forgiveness of sin and acceptance with God. Those who endure in this faith to the end will be eternally saved.

Faith is not a personal achievement or an act that earns salvation; it is a work of the Holy Spirit, by which one relies on the merits of Christ for forgiveness and eternal life. Only through such faith do sinners receive the comfort that God is gracious to them (Rom. 3:2–28; John 3:16–17; Acts 4:12; 1 Cor. 12:3).

Conversion

Conversion to faith in Christ is not brought about by human effort, conduct, or cooperation, but solely by the regenerating work of the Spirit. He brings forth repentance and faith by working through the Word. In grace He is willing to work conversion in all hearers of the Word, and those who remain unconverted are lost because of their resistance (1 Peter 1:1–4, 23; John 3:5–6; Acts 7:51).

The Christian Life

Those who are justified have become the children of God. They live in a new and reconciled relationship with Him. By the new creation God makes them able and willing to lead a holy life. They are sanctified and receive the Holy Spirit, who empowers them to serve God and the neighbor in love (Eph. 2:10; 2 Cor. 5:17; Rom. 8).

Christians are not justified by works, but by faith alone, yet faith is active in works. These works are imperfect because of the sinful flesh, but they are nevertheless covered by the perfect righteousness of Jesus. Their works are acceptable and pleasing to God for His sake. Christians do strive for perfection and have the sure hope of being sinless in the life eternal (Phil. 3:8–9; Rom. 7:21–24; Matt. 5:48; 2 Peter 3:13).

The Gospel of justification through faith alone brings Christian liberty. We are freed from slavery to sin and to burdensome notions of salvation through works. This includes liberation from the demand to use human laws and rules to please God and to gain a right relation with Him. Therefore the sanctified Christian life flows from faith and love according to God's will as revealed in His Word (Gal. 3:10–11; 5:1–6; Col. 2:18–22).

The Means of Grace

How does God offer and bestow the spiritual blessings secured by Christ, such as the forgiveness of sins and the Holy Spirit? The means He uses are called the *means of grace.* God has ordained only three means of grace: the *Gospel* (Acts 20:24, 32; Rom. 10:17; John 20:22–23); *Baptism* (Titus 3:5); and the *Lord's Supper* (Matt. 26:28; 1 Cor. 10:16). The church is not to try to use other means for this work.

The Gospel is the gracious message of salvation through Christ Jesus. Through it the Holy Spirit works to offer freely to sinners the righteousness that is in Christ and to create faith in Him (Rom. 1:16–17; 10:6–17; 1 Cor. 6:11).

The sacraments are external means connected with God's Word, through which God offers, conveys, and seals to us the grace that Christ has merited. One is Baptism, a washing of regeneration in the Holy Spirit. It works forgiveness of sins, delivers from death and the devil, and gives eternal salvation to all who believe this. At the same time it is a sign of the new life that it ushers in, indicating that the Old Adam in us should by daily contrition and repentance be drowned and die with all sins and evil lusts, and again a new man daily come forth and arise to live before God in righteousness and purity forever (Acts 2:38; Titus 3:5; Rom. 6:3–4).

The Sacrament of the Altar, or the Lord's Supper, is the body and blood of Jesus Christ, which is really present under bread and wine, for Christians to eat and to drink. Forgiveness of sins, life, and salvation are given through the words: "Given and shed for you for the forgiveness of sins" to all who receive the Supper with faith in these words (Luke 22:19–20).

The Church

One holy Christian church exists on earth, one that will continue forever. It is the fellowship of those, and only those, who believe in Christ as their Savior—those who therefore are justified and are blessed with its benefits for His sake. It is gathered, sustained, and preserved by the means of grace (Eph. 2:19; 5:25–27; Matt. 28:19–20; Acts 20:32).

The members of this fellowship possess all the spiritual rights and privileges with which Christ has endowed His church. They may exercise these rights and privileges—in general, privately—according to His will(1 Peter 2:9; Rev. 1:5–6; 1 Cor. 3:21–22). They are also to exercise them in providing for the public administration of the means of grace. They do this by calling men into the office of the holy ministry, which God has instituted for the service of the church. The church members owe the bearer of this office unconditional obedience in all things when such obedience involves obeying the Word of God itself, though never when the pastor goes beyond the Word (Titus 1:5–9; Heb. 13:17; Titus 1:13–14; 1 Peter 4:11).

The government of the church must follow the principle that Christ is its sole head and God's Word—Holy Scripture—is the sole authority to be applied for its good order. According to that Word congregations are formed, their called ministers administer the means of grace, and the redeemed people of God have a royal priesthood to exercise. The church may not set aside God's commands. It cannot speak with divine authority where the Word of God is silent (Eph. 1:22–23; Matt. 28:19–20; 2 Tim. 3:16–17; 1 Cor. 14:40; Matt. 18:17–20; Eph. 4:11; 1 Peter 2:9).

The consciences of Christians have a right to Christian liberty from subjection to human laws and creations. For example, they are not bound to regard any human organizations—such as synods or hierarchies of bishops—as necessary for the church's existence or service to God (Titus 1:14; Matt. 15:9; Eph. 2:19–22; 1 Cor. 3:11).

The activity of the church must not be confused with that of the state. God works through the church to save human beings and lead them to eternal life. To do this He makes use of the means given to the church and its ministers, namely, the Word of God and the sacraments. But through the state He aims to maintain external order. The means for accomplishing this are civil laws, compulsion, and punishment. Therefore the church and the state should not adopt each other's aims or try to do their works by employing each other's means (John 18:11, 36; 2 Cor. 10:4; 1 Tim. 2:2; Rom. 13:4).

Election

Lutherans believe in an election of grace. God predestines the elect to eternal life. They do not receive this on the basis of their merits, works, faith, or conduct, but solely because of God's grace and the merits of Christ. Believers receive great comfort knowing that God has elected them from eternity and planned to bring them to faith in Christ, justify them, sanctify them, keep them, in faith, and ultimately glorify them (Rom. 8:28–30; 2 Tim. 1:9).

Lutherans hold that God has not desired the damnation of anyone or predestined anyone to be lost. Rather God offers salvation in the Gospel even to all who are lost. Then why are some saved and others not saved? God has not revealed a solution for this mystery. He has revealed that He is not the cause of anyone's damnation and that humanity is not the cause of election to salvation. (1 Tim. 2:3–4; Ezek. 33:11; Matt. 23:37; 1 Tim. 1:9)

The Return of Christ

On the Last Day Christ will come visibly to judge the world. To all who believe on Him He will give the eternal life and glory that He has gained as the Redeemer (Acts 1:11; 1 Thess. 4:16–17; John 14:19). They will forever behold Him in His glory (John 17:24) and praise Him that He "was slain and has redeemed us to God by His blood" (Rev. 5:9). But on those who do not acknowledge Him He will pronounce the doom of everlasting punishment. All the bodies of the dead will be raised to take part in one of these destinies (Matt. 25:31–46).

Lutheran Worship

The justification of the sinner by grace through faith in Christ lies at the center of Lutheran worship and church rites. The worship service contains an address of God to His people. He offers and conveys His grace in the Gospel (the preaching of the Word and the Absolution), Baptism, and the Lord's Supper. The people of God are blessed, and instruction takes place for their edification in the life in Christ. They are also given liturgical opportunities to respond to God in praise of His grace and devotion of themselves to Him.

Lutheran worship is, if consistent, permeated with the spirit of Christian liberty in the Gospel. It uses the freedom to employ a multitude of allowable public and private customs to serve the proclamation of the Gospel and give order to the Christians' response to it. Examples are hymns, chants, altars, pulpits, offerings, set forms of prayers, the sign of the cross, the observance of the church year, confirmation, and the like. However, ceremonies and customs that express false doctrine or give false impressions about Christianity are not proper uses of Christian liberty.

Something to Think About

1. Why is our church often called the "Evangelical Lutheran Church"?

2. What does the term *Lutheran Symbols* mean? Why is this important? List the Symbols, giving a sentence to describe each one.

3. We teach that the Lutheran Confessions do not *supplement* the Scriptures. Why is that important? What does it imply about our view of Scripture?

4. The Lutheran Confessions are "normed by Scripture." What does that mean?

5. What difference does it make if pastors pledge agreement with the Lutheran Confessions "because they agree with Scripture," rather than "insofar as they agree"?

6. What quotation from the Lutheran Confessions, contained in this chapter, expresses the thought of Gal. 1:8?

7. Christ has traded places with us. For example, He gave us the benefits of His perfect obedience, and He took the punishment for our sins. Some call this the "happy exchange." What else did Christ exchange for us?

8. Why is Oct. 31, 1517, celebrated as the beginning of the Reformation?

9. Explain the distinction between Law and Gospel.

10. Is either of these statements true? (a) Good works are necessary for salvation. (b) Good works are necessary.

11. What does Christian liberty mean to you?

12. What are the means of grace?

13. Why is there joy in being a member of Christ's church?

14. What comfort does the doctrine of election provide?

15. What does the Lutheran church teach about church and state?

=
3
=
Ancient Traditions

Eastern Orthodoxy and Roman Catholicism have a history and a tradition that reaches back to the early days of the church. Since they both claim to possess teaching that is catholic (authoritative throughout the whole world), they are often called the Eastern Catholics and the Roman Catholics.

Eastern Orthodoxy

Eastern Orthodoxy is a communion of churches sharing a tradition of doctrine and worship. Orthodox churches have organized into bodies along nationalistic lines, such as Greek, Serbian, and Romanian. Immigrants to the United States have established daughter churches of the bodies in their homelands. The largest are the Greek Orthodox and the Orthodox Church in America (which has Russian roots).

The Orthodox churches are independent bodies. But they consider themselves to be in communion with the Patriarch of Constantinople, whom they honor as the chief bishop (the Ecumenical Patriarch) of Orthodoxy.

They are called *Orthodox* ("right-teaching") because of their claim to be conserving the correct and apostolic teaching of Christianity. "Eastern" indicates that Christians once operated under a united organization. It suffered the schism between East and West (1054), which has never healed. This was caused by doctrinal and political strife. The churches mutually excommunicated the Roman Catholic pope and the Patriarch of Constantinople. In modern times the two groups have been moving closer together.

This Greek symbol is common in Orthodox symbolism. It is formed from the letters Chi Rho in Christos, the Greek title of the Messiah (Anointed King). The Chi is tilted to show the Savior's cross, and the Alpha and Omega are added to proclaim that He is the everlasting God. (See Matt. 16:16; Rev. 1:8; 22:13–16.) The symbol sums up Orthodoxy's teaching about Christ. It is an example of how much there is to commend in the Orthodox tradition (e.g., the Trinity, the incarnation of God, His atoning sacrifice, and the hope of eternal life).

Source of Doctrine

The source of doctrine in Eastern Orthodoxy is Holy Scripture (in which Tobit, Judith, Sirach, and other apocryphal books are included) and the oral tradition of Christ and His apostles. Eastern Orthodoxy teaches that tradition completes and explains Scripture. It is equally inspired and necessary.

Since the church is "the pillar and foundation of the truth" (1 Tim. 3:15), it is thought to have the gift of infallibly, preserving and interpreting Scripture and oral tradition. The gift belongs to the church as a whole, being exercised when the bishops of the church speak together. The Orthodox consider it an arrogant presumption for the pope of Rome or any individual bishop to claim infallibility.

The church spoke as a whole in the seven ecumenical (worldwide church) councils. Two were held at Nicea (325; 787), three at Constantinople (381; 553; 681), one at Ephesus (431), and one at Chalcedon (451). The most esteemed council decree is the Nicene Creed. Apostolic tradition has also been preserved in writings of church fathers, regional church councils, individual bishops, and theologians. But these do not have a guarantee of infallible freedom from human opinion. Therefore the Orthodox sometimes differ among themselves over statements found in these writings.

The Orthodox use these sources to judge the correctness of teachings and teachers. The most famous example is their opposition to the phrase "and the Son," which Western Christendom added to the Nicene Creed ("I believe in the Holy Spirit, ... who proceeds from the Father and the Son"). The Orthodox assert that this phrase cannot be proved from either Scripture or tradition. (But see Gal. 4:6; Rom. 8:4; 1 Peter 1:11; and John 16:15.)

It would be dangerous and distressing if it were really true that Scripture is not complete and sufficient, or that church teachings must be accepted even if they are not found in Scripture. (See 2 Tim. 3:16; Acts 17:11; and Luke 16:31.)

The words of 1 Tim. 3:15 mean simply that the Christian church possesses the truth in the Word of God.

Why should we not consider the apocryphal books to be part of the Bible? They contain no statement that they came into existence as inspired prophetical writings. They were simply pious religious literature. The New Testament does not use them as norms of teaching. Luther included them in his Bible translation under the heading: "Books that are not to be held equal to the Holy Scriptures but nevertheless are useful and good to read."

Statements of the Eastern Orthodox Heritage

We identify the traditional teaching of Orthodoxy by consulting the ecumenical councils, regional councils, and church fathers, as well as the confessions of faith, catechisms, and theological books used by that communion through the centuries. The Confession of Dositheus is often quoted to show the Orthodox heritage.

The Way of Salvation

According to Orthodoxy, humanity is fallen and corrupt, but not dead in sin. We have a will that is free to cooperate with God in bringing about our conversion and justification. Jesus' death for sinners brought forgiveness and opened the way to salvation. But one must be justified by becoming righteous in a life of works and so receive eternal life as a reward. "We believe that man is justified not simply by faith alone, but by faith which is active through love, that is, through faith and works" (Confession of Dositheus, XIII. This is contrary to God's Word in Rom. 3:28 and Eph. 2:8–9.)

The Sacraments

The Orthodox believe that God enables people to do the meritorious works that deserve eternal life. He has instituted sacraments in which grace is transmitted for this purpose. As in Roman Catholicism, the Orthodox teach seven sacraments: Baptism, Confirmation or Chrismation (from the Greek word for the holy oil used in it), the Eucharist, Penance, Holy Orders, Matrimony, and the Anointing of the Sick. (Lutherans point out that Scripture contains an institution for only three of these as means of grace—Matt. 28:19; 1 Cor. 11:23–29; John 20:22–23.)

The proper method of Baptism in orthodox tradition is said to be threefold immersion: Baptism, Chrismation (anointing with oil), and the Eucharist are given to children at the same time.

Leavened bread is used in Holy Communion because of a belief that Jesus used it. The Orthodox practice intinction; pieces of bread soaked in wine are administered to the people, usually on a spoon. The Orthodox teach that the bread and wine change into the body and blood of Christ. However, they do not commit themselves to the Roman Catholic philosophical explanation of this. The Orthodox use the Eucharist to offer the sacrifice of the mass, in which they claim to join Christ in making the atoning sacrifice for their sins.

The Orthodox usually do not teach that God requires a Christian to make satisfaction or payment for sin, either in penance or in a purgatory after this life. They allow their priests to be married. While stressing the sanctity of marriage, they recognize the ground for divorce mentioned in Matt. 19:9.

The Church

According to Orthodoxy, the church is the community instituted by Christ to preach His Word, promote union with Himself, and lead believers to eternal life. Christ ordained a necessary form of government for it, in which the office of the bishop is central. As the Confession of Dositheus (found in Leith, *Creeds of the Churches*) puts it, "The office of a bishop is so essential that without it there could be no church nor any Christians. The bishop stands in uninterrupted apostolic succession, a living image of God on earth" (X).

Since only Orthodoxy has properly preserved the form of government, it claims that it alone is the church, strictly speaking. The church is the visible body of Christ, consisting of all who are governed by the bishops, both believers and hypocrites. Believers outside of Orthodoxy can have saving grace, but they are not visibly in the church Christ founded. Whether they are in it in some other way continues to be discussed.

This conception about bishops and the visible body of the church has no support in Scripture. It is a misleading teaching about how to be sure we are in the Savior's church.

Orthodox Churches and Their Worship

Note the architecture typical of some Orthodox churches, with onion-shaped cupola and the Russian cross. The cross has three bars. The top bar represents the superscription on Jesus' cross, and the bottom bar is wrenched out of kilter to represent the agony of Good Friday.

This model illustrates the nature of the worship in Orthodox churches. Words, music, gestures, objects, vestments, and architecture portray God's activity in past and present. Worship has the central emphasis in Orthodoxy. The liturgy is a religious drama that presents the doctrines of the church and the history of humanity's salvation. In it the worshiper glorifies God, receives sacramental grace for justification, and offers prayers and the sacrifice of the mass.

Adoration and prayer are made to saints to implore their intercession for blessing on the worshiper's efforts toward justification. Icons (holy pictures) of saints are considered to be valuable aids in prayers to saints.

Icons are commonly found in homes and on the iconostasis screen in churches. The people adore them, kiss them, and offer candles and incense to them. Besides being helpful reminders and encouragements for faith, icons bring the worshiper into close association with the persons depicted. The saint depicted is truly present in the icon and united with it, so that the adoration of it becomes adoration of him or her.

But the Word of God forbids us to give adoration and prayer to creatures, whether persons or things (Ex. 20:5; Matt. 4:10).

Roman Catholicism

The Roman Catholic Church, often known as "the Catholic Church," or simply "Rome," is the largest denomination in America and in the world. Its head, the pope, has his headquarters in the Vatican in Rome. The word *catholic* indicates the claim that it is the universal church founded by Christ and that all other denominations are merely man-made sects. Its ancient tradition contains and uses the teachings and concepts that are part of the history of Christianity—both biblical truths and human additions that other denominations accept or have rejected.

Source of Doctrine

Like Eastern Orthodoxy, Rome draws its teaching from both Scripture (including the apocryphal books) and oral tradition as preserved in ancient writings. Rome asserts that the church has infallible authority to identify, express, and interpret the divine teaching in this twofold revelation. The Bible is obscure and ambiguous if not used in the light of tradition and the authoritative interpretation of the church. It is easy, then, for the church to become the source of its own teaching. Reason and revelation are said to support each other, and doctrines are shaped (opponents will say distorted, as in Rome's doctrine of justification) to show that they are reasonable.

The authority of the church to establish doctrine can be expressed in two ways: when the whole church speaks in an ecumenical council; and when the pope teaches as the head of the church, the Vicar (or Representative) of Christ. The statements of popes and councils are infallible when they are formal teachings of faith or morals and are stated with an intention that they be binding on the church in an irrevocable way. Roman theologians sometimes disagree on whether a particular statement of a pope or council is to be regarded as infallible or simply as official in a more tentative way.

Statements of the Roman Catholic Heritage

The doctrines of the Roman church are found in the (officially approved) ecumenical creeds, the decisions of its 21 ecumenical councils, the authorized catechisms and declarations, the pope's communications and letters, and the official liturgical publications. These contain standards for teaching and church discipline. The best known of them are the documents of the Council of Trent (1545–63) and the Second Vatican Council (1962–65).

Pluralism

Official Roman Catholic doctrine can be outlined, as we have seen. But a wide range of conflicting ideas and schools of thought exist. The church has long allowed controversial views—for example, the theory of evolution, or historical criticism of the Bible—as long as they are not judged to conflict with the infallible teachings of the church.

The range of what is allowable has continued to expand as the doctrinal statements have been reinterpreted by means of distinctions between unalterable "truths" and "changeable conceptions" in them. This means that "diverse theological formulations are often to be considered as mutually complementary rather than conflicting" (Decree on Ecumenism of the Second Vatican Council, 17).

All this has led to dissension between traditionalists and progressives on matters like the deity of Christ and universalism (the idea that all will be saved). Some go even further, questioning the concept of infallibility of popes and councils.

The Way of Salvation

Roman Catholics traditionally hold many Christian concepts with which we agree, such as the Trinity, the Incarnation, the Fall, original sin, the Atonement (Jesus made an atonement for fallen and sinful humanity by His perfect life and death on the cross, in order to bring about reconciliation), grace (God's favor and gifts, necessary for Salvation), and the means of grace (means by which God bestows saving grace on people to redeem and sanctify them—the Word of God and the Sacraments). Nevertheless, serious differences exist about the way of salvation.

Conversion

Conversion, Rome teaches, is helped by the efforts of a person's natural will. Grace is the necessary help that God provides so that fallen people can use their inborn powers to play their part in conversion.

Note the contrast: Scripture teaches that natural, unconverted people are spiritually blind, dead, and enemies of God. Romanism, however, pictures humans as sick and weakened, but with some powers remaining, powers that can be strengthened and invigorated by a physician.

How Your Debt of Sin Is Paid

According to Rome:

>   *Received from Christ* x
>
>   *Received from you* y
>
>   *Paid in full by joint payment* $x + y$

According to Scripture:

>   *Received from Christ* x
>
>   *Received from you* 0
>
>   *Paid in Full by Christ Alone* x

See Gal. 3:10–13 and Rom. 3:10–25.

Justification

In modern discussions and dialogs Roman Catholics emphasize faith in Christ and affirm that no one can be saved without grace. Many people conclude that Lutherans have sadly misunderstood the Catholics and that Catholics teach pretty much the same as Lutherans do about salvation.

However, Roman Catholics still teach that justification means that God gives sinners a saving righteousness—a righteousness that *they can use to help themselves* in the face of God's condemnation of them for their sin. That righteousness is an inherent righteousness, or moral holiness, that God creates in them by an act of renewal.

Because of this righteousness God is reconciled to the sinner. This saving righteousness is not the perfect obedience of Christ. In the 16th century the Council of Trent (Sixth Session) denounced the teaching that we are forgiven and justified solely for the sake of what Christ has done. Rome sees Christ's obedience as the basis on which God gives us our own righteousness, not as Christ's righteousness given to us (Rom. 1:17).

Catholicism makes a distinction between the initial reception of the saving righteousness and the preservation and increase of that righteousness so that Christians can complete their justification and earn its outcome, eternal life. The initial righteousness comes to the baby when it is baptized and to the non-Christian adult who is converted. This does not bring eternal life. Rather, it opens us to the possibility and opportunity to merit eternal life by good works. The saving righteousness is made evident and increased by doing good works to merit more and more grace (divine help) and eternal life.

To Catholics the statement "Man is justified by grace" means that the initial reception of righteousness is not merited by good works and that God graciously assists people to merit eternal life. "Man is justified by good works" means that saving righteousness is received and maintained by good works. "Man is justified by faith" means that people believe that God's grace and Christ's work will help them merit eternal life. The doctrine of Trent has never been given up—but was reaffirmed—at Vatican II.

This doctrine disagrees with Scripture (Rom. 3:24). As Trent itself affirms (Sixth Session, Chapter IX), this doctrine makes it impossible for individuals to have undoubtable certainty that they really are justified.

We see an application of this doctrine of justification by works in the concept of "anonymous Christianity" taught by the Second Vatican Council (Dogmatic Constitution on the Church, 16). That is, people can be justified anonymously, without using the name of Jesus, if they live a life of love and good will toward their neighbors and have a spirit of hope. These are signs that saving grace is working in their lives, though they do not realize it.

Thus, Rome teaches justification by good works or good qualities in people. But the Bible teaches that one can be justified only by trusting in what Jesus has done for sinners. St. Peter said that salvation depends on the name of Jesus. "There is no other name under heaven given to men by which we must be saved" (Acts 4:12).

Satisfaction for Sin

Rome teaches that forgiveness for sin is given because of Jesus' suffering and death, but sinners must still make satisfaction for sins—by acts of punishment that make amends to the majesty of God offended by sin.

Scripture rejects this teaching. We could never pay God back adequately for our offenses against Him. Jesus paid all the debt of our sin for us on the cross. This is credited to us as if we had done it ourselves. "He was pierced for our transgressions, He was crushed for our iniquities; the punishment that brought us peace was upon Him, and by His wounds we are healed.... The Lord has laid on Him the iniquity of us all" (Is. 53:5–6).

We don't need to add works of satisfaction to that. God freely gives us full forgiveness. For the same reason we reject the idea that there is a purgatory, where payment for sin is made by suffering.

The Papal Seal

This seal shows the pope's crown surmounted by a globe to show his claim to world kingship as the Vicar of Christ. The keys signify his claim to power over the gates of the kingdom of heaven.

According to Rome, the papacy has been instituted by God to be the head of the church. This is based on Matt. 16:18, which is also interpreted to mean that the pope is infallible in all that he teaches officially as the head of the church in matters of faith and morals.

Papal monarchy is one way in which the church can be organized, and we would not object to it if the popes faithfully held to biblical teachings. But we must object to the claim that God instituted this office and that the pope, therefore, must be the head of the Christian church. That is not taught in Matt. 16:18 ("You are Peter, and on this rock I will build My church") or elsewhere in Scripture. The rock on which the church is built is Jesus Christ Himself (Luke 20:17; Acts 4:11) and the truth about Him (Matt. 16:16). Peter's name refers to the testimony he gives to the fact that Christ is the rock of the church.

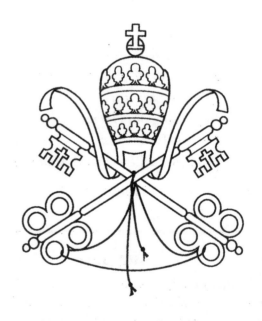

The bodies known as the Old Catholics have become separate from the Church of Rome because of this teaching. They agree with much of its theology but do not accept the pope's claim to infallibility and the divine right to rule the church.

The Church

Both Roman Catholics and Lutherans teach that Jesus Christ has founded the holy Christian church through His apostles and commissioned it to preach His Gospel to the nations, and that He is present with His people in it to forgive and save and sanctify them. Also, He has instituted the office of the holy ministry (or of the pastor), into which men should be called to preach His Word and administer the sacraments in His name. Christians must obey their pastor when such obedience involves obeying the Word of God itself.

Catholicism says that the Christian church is a body of people who profess faith in Christ and are governed by bishops and the pope. The government of bishops is part of God's will for the church and must be included in the definition of the church.

Lutherans disagree. The church is the body of all who believe in Christ as Savior. It is found wherever there are Christians, no matter what form of church government they use. Some Lutherans have a system of bishops; some don't. But all agree that the Word of God does not require government by bishops. Forms of church government have developed historically. Some form is necessary for the church to exist. The formation of congregations and the office of the ministry, on the other hand, are divinely instituted and are necessary.

Rome teaches that only those ministers who are ordained by bishops are truly in the office of the ministry. The office must be bestowed by bishops in the succession of the apostles. Therefore the Roman Catholic Church does not consider Lutheran ministers to be real pastors before God and does not think that the Lutheran church has valid Absolutions or valid Eucharists.

Scripture teaches that any man called by a congregation to preach the Word and administer the sacraments has the office of the ministry, even though the ordination that confirms this call does not have any Roman Catholic bishops acting in it. Lutheran pastors are not ordinarily called priests, because they do not have the function of offering sacrifice, which the Old Testament priests had and which Roman priests also have.

The Sacraments

According to Rome, people are justified by grace that enables them to do meritorious works. Sacraments are outward signs instituted by Christ to infuse that grace. Each of the seven sacraments gives sanctifying grace

---

The Sacrifice of the Mass

Lutherans do not accept the teaching that the body and blood of Christ in Holy Communion can be used as a sacrifice to offer up to God. The Savior offered His body as a sacrifice on Good Friday. In Holy Communion He gives us that body and all the benefits obtained in His sacrifice. But we cannot join Him in offering sacrifice for our sins. We cannot add our sacrifices to His. He has made His sacrifice once for all on the cross, and it is not repeated in the Lord's Supper.

---

for the performance of good works to achieve justification. In addition, each supplies a special grace for meeting one of the needs of the spiritual life: rebirth (Baptism), growth (Confirmation), nourishment (Holy Communion), cure for sin after Baptism (Penance), married life (Matrimony), work of the church (Ordination), and strength in dying weakness (Anointing of the Sick).

Baptism

This Sacrament gives forgiveness and also wipes out the very essence of original sin, so that the corruption that remains is not truly sin.

Confirmation

Confirmation strengthens Christians by bestowing a gift of the Holy Spirit to make them soldiers of Christ.

The Eucharist

Real presence is explained by the theory that the consecrating priest has the power to change the substance of bread and wine into the body and blood of Christ, though appearances of bread and wine remain. (But God says that bread remains, 1 Cor. 11:27.) Since the Middle Ages Rome has mandated the practice of withholding the wine from the laity, though Vatican II has provided for exceptions in modern times. (But the "exception" should be the rule—Christ's rule, Matt. 26:27.)

Penance

Penance is the sacrament that gives remission of the guilt and punishment for sins committed after Baptism. These are obtained by works of contrition, confession, and satisfaction for sin. There are two kinds of sinful acts: mortal sins (serious offenses deserving eternal punishment) and venial sins (slighter offenses deserving only temporal punishments, lasting for a time). According to the church law of Rome, only a priest can remit mortal sins (Council of Trent, Session XIV). Grace and forgiveness can be directly received from God by an act of contrition, but only if this is done in a right spirit, a spirit that will later be willing to go to confession or penance.

The priest's absolution takes away guilt and eternal punishment, but sinners must make satisfaction for the temporal punishments required for their sins. In penance a priest requires works. Divine justice can also be satisfied through prayer, the mass, fasting, merciful acts, and patient suffering in this life and after death in purgatory. The church also provides indulgences, which are reductions or remissions of temporal punishment. They can be earned by prayers, Bible study and teaching, and other works. Indulgences make various amounts of cancellation of punishment available, but the amount actually taken away depends on one's moral effort.

Certainly absolution should be honored as a means of grace through which God forgives sins (Matt. 16:19; 18:18; John 20:23). But the following are also true: (1) The removal of the curse of damnation is needed for all sins (Gal. 3:10). (2) Scripture does not teach that forgiveness depends on confession to a priest. (3) We obtain forgiveness solely through faith that Jesus Christ was punished for our sins in our place; we do not do good works for the purpose of satisfaction and reconciliation with God (Rom. 3:23–28; Matt. 27:46; 2 Cor. 5:15, 19).

Matrimony

The Roman Church honors the divine institution of marriage and rightly teaches the duty of husband and wife to be faithful to each other. But some of its marriage laws have no basis in Scripture. For example, the marriage of a Roman Catholic is said to be invalid if done before a justice of the peace.

Holy Orders

Ordination, it is taught, bestows the power to administer sacraments in a way that enables them to have the desired effect. Priests could change bread and wine into Christ's body and blood and offer the Sacrifice of the Mass. Ordination imprints an indelible character on the priest's soul.

Anointing of the Sick

Also known as Extreme Unction or the Last Rites, this is a ceremony with holy oil and prayer for the seriously ill. It gives health and strength to the soul and sometimes to the body.

Veneration of Saints

Roman Catholics interpret Matt. 4:10 to allow the worship of saints with oblation and prayer if they are given the worship that belongs to God. Roman Catholics believe saints have such great merits that they can obtain benefits for us through their intercessions. The Virgin Mary has the most merit, as indicated in the famous prayer: "O Mary, conceived without sin, pray for us who have recourse to thee."

Something to Think About

1. How does it help you to know that Scripture alone is the source of doctrine, not Scripture plus the oral tradition of Christ and His apostles?

2. Compare the Eastern Orthodox and Roman Catholic teachings about the church. Explain the statement from this chapter about such a teaching: It is a misleading instruction about how to find certainty of being in the Savior's church.

3. What is the papacy? What claims are made about it? What attitude do you take toward these claims?

4. Explain the way of salvation as the Orthodox teach it. How does it disagree with Scripture?

5. What are some problems with the teaching that sinners must make satisfaction for their sins?

6. Contrast Lutheran and Roman Catholic definitions of *grace*.

7. Why are sacraments important in the Orthodox and Roman Catholic concepts about the way of salvation? List their seven sacraments. Show from the Bible which of these have been instituted by God as a means of grace.

8. Why is it wrong to pray to saints?

9. Contrast Roman Catholic and Lutheran teaching about the Lord's Supper.

10. What is pluralism? Explain why the Roman Catholic Church allows pluralism.

11. What is "anonymous Christianity"?

= 4 = Churches of the Calvinist Reformation

John Calvin

The name Calvinistic will be used here to refer to churches that have carried on the original teaching of John Calvin (1509–64) in their traditional heritage. These are the (1) Presbyterian bodies and (2) the (European) Continental Calvinists, which use the word Reformed in their names, such as the Reformed Church in America. However, their pastors and the people of their churches are often not in full agreement with this heritage.

Statements of the Calvinist Heritage

The Westminster Confession, the Belgic Confession, the Heidelberg Catechism, and the Canons of the Council of Dort are the principal declarations used by the Calvinist churches in America. The degree to which their pastors are expected to agree with the content of these documents as standards varies according to the bodies involved.

The two largest Reformed bodies in America are the Reformed Church in America (formed in the 17th century) and the Christian Reformed Church (organized in 1857). They are both of Dutch extraction. The second has a history of being stricter in adhering to the confessional standards accepted by both groups.

The largest American Presbyterian body is the Presbyterian Church (U.S.A.), formed in 1983. It was actually a reunion of the older Presbyterian group in the country with a Southern body that had splintered off from it at the time of the Civil War.

Historically, the ordination vows of American Presbyterians required subscription to the Westminster Confession and its catechisms "as containing the system of doctrine taught in the Holy Scripture." Controversy often existed over how many teachings belonged to that "system" and whether the Westminster Confession and Catechisms contained teachings to which subscription was not required—either because they were not found in Scripture, or because they were not considered inspired and infallible.

A major controversy dealt with (1) the verbal inspiration of the Bible, (2) the virgin birth of Christ, (3) the vicarious atonement, (4) the bodily resurrection of Christ, and (5) His power to do miracles.

The General Assembly of the Northern Presbyterians required all subscribers to teach all five as belonging to the system of doctrine (1910, 1923). Liberals protested in the Auburn Affirmation (1924) and eventually won the right to teach dissenting views. When the modernistic Confession of 1967 was added to the confessional documents of the Northern Presbyterians, the new confession virtually went down the line of the doctrinal paragraphs of the Auburn Affirmation.

Doctrines of the Calvinistic Heritage

The Calvinistic heritage affirms many of the same doctrines that Lutherans do, such as the Trinity, the incarnation of Christ, the divine authority of Scripture (but not of tradition), and justification by Christ's righteousness being credited to us. Some differences occur in the following areas.

Salvation by Grace

The Reformed teach the total depravity of humanity and the necessity of saving grace, unconditional election, and the atonement of Christ. We cannot simply identify Reformed theology with synergism (cooperating with God in our salvation), because it is not true of strict Calvinist Reformed tradition. But synergism occurs among the Reformed who have been influenced by Arminianism. Traditional Calvinism is typically expressed in the Westminster Confession of the Presbyterians:

> Man, by his fall into a state of sin, hath wholly lost all ability of will to any spiritual good accompanying salvation.... When God converts a sinner, and translates him into the state of grace, he freeth him from his natural bondage under sin, and by his grace alone enables him freely to will and to do that which is spiritually good. (IX:3–4)

A Calvinist can appreciate the story of the man who said that his conversion was due to himself and to God: "I fought against God with all my might, and He did the rest." His conversion was not due to himself at all.

The Westminster Confession (and the Calvinist tradition) goes on to say that God has unconditionally—that is, not on the basis of any foreknown conduct—predestinated some to salvation and some to damnation. According to this teaching, saving grace is not universal (worldwide in scope). God has decided not even to offer it to part of the human race; it was never intended for them. The predamned are those whom He and His grace pass by.

Most traditional Calvinists hold that the atonement of Christ had infinite value and so was sufficient in itself to save the whole human race. But, they continue, Christ's purpose in dying was only to make atonement for the elect (Westminster Confession VIII:5). The atonement is based on the divine decree to elect some.

In accord with a limited atonement, saving grace is also limited and selective—only intended for and offered to a part of humanity. Such teaching considers universal grace, as taught by Lutherans and others, to be in error.

The call to believe and be saved is extended to both elect and nonelect. Reformed theologians call it an earnest, sincere, and serious offer. But they do not mean that it is a serious, earnest offer to every human being to give him or her what Christ has obtained for them. Calvinists offer no serious Gospel for the nonelect. The call addressed to the nonelected person is serious merely in the sense of a serious proclamation of the conditions to be fulfilled for salvation—that is, of the general promise to save all who believe in Christ.

This point is important for evangelism, as we can see in the statements of the strictest Calvinists about that subject. According to them, one must not say to the unconverted sinner, "Christ died for you," but "Christ died for sinners." We cannot know whether the one addressed belongs to the group of intended beneficiaries. The elect who hear the invitation will be enlightened, so they know the Good News refers to them.

Calvinist theology also teaches that saving grace is irresistible; it is the grace of the sovereign God, and perpetual perseverance in grace is given to everyone who is converted. A person who has been converted cannot fall from grace or lose the Holy Spirit. The rule is "once saved, always saved."

These opinions of limited atonement and irresistible grace are still held among Calvinists today, especially in the smaller bodies. But a large number of the heirs of Calvin have long recognized that such teachings are not scriptural.

The Means of Grace

Unfortunately, the doctrine of immediate grace (the belief that forgiveness and life are bestowed without the means of Word and Sacrament) leads people to look for evidence of grace in their own feelings, attitudes, and works. They want to see if that immediate grace has come to them and worked and that they truly are regenerated, have forgiveness, and are children of God. This is the point, for instance, of Articles XIV, XV, and XVI of the Westminster Confession. The subjects of these articles (faith, repentance, and good works) are regarded as the effects of immediate grace. Therefore one must base assurance of having saving grace on the experience of these things. This explains what the Westminster Confession says about good works: "By them believers ... strengthen their assurance" (Article XVI). This doctrine does not teach that people are justified by good works, or that good works and activities of repentance earn justification, but that these are the grounds of assurance.

This is a problem for all who teach immediate grace. The problem becomes more severe if people hold the orthodox Calvinist position that grace is not for all people. Then individuals need to try to convince themselves that saving grace was intended for them in the first place. They are not allowed to say, "Grace is offered to all, therefore it must be also available to me." So they must look at their repentance, faith, and good works, their moods and inner experiences, to see if they feel like they have grace.

Scripture teaches that we can and should use the means of grace to receive what they offer and bestow. We do not simply use them to prepare us to get the blessings in some other way alongside the means of grace. The Larger Westminster Catechism of the Presbyterians states that the means of grace are the Word, sacraments, and prayer (under question 154). It views prayer as a means instituted by God by which believers can express and exercise their faith to obtain blessings. It sees Word and Sacraments as means of grace in the same sense as prayer is.

The Calvinistic explanation of the Law as a means of grace is particularly disturbing. This leads to an overemphasis on the Law and a confusion of the Law with the Gospel. Heb. 12:14 ("without holiness no one will see the Lord") should not be taken to mean that the Law is a means of grace or a condition for securing God's favor. It means that faith is necessary for salvation and refers to the holy life as the fruit of that faith, by which it may be identified.

The Calvinistic misconceptions about the Law and the relation of grace to means are often reflected in statements about seeking assurance of salvation. They may say that genuine assurance comes from seeing the Holy Spirit's transforming work in one's life, or that unconditional surrender to God is the essence of saving faith.

Such ideas compromise the doctrine of the free gift of grace and mix the comfort of acceptance with thoughts and questions about obligations.

The Application of Grace

Calvinists teach that regeneration, forgiveness, life, and salvation are not brought about by means—not by action of the Word, or Baptism, or the Supper—but by the action of the Spirit. But Calvinists, Anglicans, Baptists, and other Protestants do use the term "means of grace."

As a matter of fact, some Calvinist theology books have a chapter headed, "The Means of Grace." But they do not define these as means of conferring benefits that bring about faith to receive the benefits. They say that means of grace stir up faith to seek the benefits from God directly. They are aids to faith. They do not have inherent power, by the Spirit working in them, to give and bestow the benefits.

Calvinists often compare the Word of God and the sacraments to light: These are means of grace as light is a means of vision. It does not have the power to make the blind eye see, but is the means by which a healthy eye can exercise its sight. The Reformed conceive of means of grace as ways by which the Spirit exerts influence on those who have been regenerated by immediate grace. They are means of further development and sanctification.

Christ

Calvinists believe that the incarnation of Christ is the basis of the Atonement. The God-man came both to be a divine Savior and to act as Substitute for sinful humanity. The Reformed—all non-Lutheran Protestants—have never accepted the doctrine of Jesus' communication of attributes (that the two natures of Jesus the God-man share each other's attributes or characteristics). They protest that a finite human nature is incapable of receiving infinite divine qualities without being exploded, or some such thing.

Probably the best-known conclusion drawn from this is the denial of the real presence of the body and blood of Christ in the Lord's Supper. The body and blood belong to Christ's human nature which, they maintain, is limited to the possibilities for finite creatures, including the inability to be in more than one place at one time. Since Christ's body has ascended into heaven, it is there until the Second Advent and cannot be present at the same time on earthly altars in the Lord's Supper. The eating and drinking of His body and blood can only be done by a mystical experience of the believing soul.

The Law

Calvinists differ from Lutherans in their understanding of the relationship between Law and Gospel. They do believe that justification is a gift of God by which the sinful person is received into God's favor and forgiven because the righteousness of Christ is credited to them. This acceptance is not earned by obeying the Law.

Calvinists view the Law as necessary in securing justification. To secure is to establish, to make sure one's status. The Law-keeping of sanctification is the basis on which the justified person receives benefits from the relationship he or she has with God. Calvinists say that "holiness, or conformity to the divine law, is the indispensable condition for securing favor, attaining peace of conscience, and enjoying fellowship with God" (Louis Berkhof, *Systematic Theology*, Eerdmans, 1941, p. 472). This, they say, is the meaning of Heb. 12:14: "Without holiness no one will see the Lord."

Calvinist writers call the Law a means of grace—for securing one's justification, strengthening one's personal assurance of being justified, and for coming into possession of the blessings of the covenant that one enjoys with God. Calvinism teaches three uses of the Law. Unlike Lutheran theology, which sees the Law as a mirror, curb, and rule, their Third Use of the Law spurs or stimulates one to attain moral righteousness. Thus, the indispensable condition for securing God's favor can be fulfilled. The Law becomes a means of sanctification by exciting and directing spiritual activity. By calling forth obedience the Law brings about sanctification and leads people in the way of life and salvation.

TULIP

The word tulip has become a common acrostic for summarizing the five points of Calvinistic theology that were declared at the Synod of Dort (1618–19) against the beliefs of Arminianism (see chapter 5). The word comes from the initial letters of five English terms describing these points.

T   otal depravity
U   nconditional predestination
L   imited atonement
I   rresistible grace
P   erseverance in grace

While this flower cannot be transplanted to a Lutheran garden, Scripture teaches some of the concepts that the letters stand for. They contain important elements of biblical truth.

T   The Calvinists rightly teach that all descendants of Adam are by nature totally corrupt in spiritual matters. People do not have freedom of the will to turn to God in faith or cooperate in their conversion (Eph. 2:1; John 3:5–6; Rom. 8:7).

U   Scripture does teach that it is by grace that God has predestinated the elect to eternal salvation and given them justifying faith. It is not because of any condition fulfilled by them (2 Tim. 1:9; Eph. 1:4–6; Phil. 1:29). However, the Bible does *not* teach, as do the Calvinists, that some are predestined for damnation. God wants *all* to be saved (1 Tim. 2:4).

L   It is true that Christ died for the church and purchased it with His blood (Eph. 5:25; Acts 20:28). Furthermore, His atoning death does not mean that all people are saved (1 Cor. 1:18). However, Jesus died for all (2 Cor. 5:15).

I   We agree that God makes us alive by His mighty power, without our aid (Eph. 2:5; John 1:13). But Scripture warns that we *can* resist God's gracious call (Matt. 23:37; Acts 7:51; 2 Cor. 6:1).

   And some people do resist God's grace, or all would be saved (1 Tim. 2:4). Furthermore, God warns us not to resist His grace (2 Cor. 6:1; Heb. 4:7).

P   We affirm with Scripture that those who are predestined to salvation cannot be lost but will continue by God's power to a blessed end (Rom. 8:30; 1 Peter 1:5). Scripture does not teach, however, that those who come to faith cannot lose that faith (Heb. 6:4–6; 10:26–29; Ps. 51:11). God urges His people not to continue in sin but to live in repentance and faith (Rom. 6:1–4).

They teach that the Gospel is good news, including the good news that the believer can use the Law as a means of grace in this way. That is, the Gospel reaffirms the Law and shows its value. It gives assurance that the believer will be enabled by God to obey the Law and acquire the blessings of salvation by doing so.

Church Government

The most traditional Calvinists follow Calvin in holding that the church must be governed by a presbyterian form of government. This means government by presbyters (a word from the Greek meaning elder). The Presbyterian churches, of course, derive their name from this term. Lay elders and teaching elders (or pastors) must conduct the affairs of the congregation and of the denominational body of congregations. This is based on their understanding of Bible passages referring to elders.

Congregationalism

Some Calvinists within the Church of England disagreed with the Presbyterian view of church government. These were the Congregationalists, so-called because they believed that the local congregation had the right to decide its affairs. Others could not require them to adhere to any statement of faith. The congregation could adopt any doctrinal platform, or none at all, as it thought best. The Congregationalists tended to hold that congregational government was the only valid form of church life.

The Pilgrims of the Plymouth Colony in Massachusetts brought Congregationalism to America. They united with the Puritans in New England under the Cambridge Platform of 1648. In this agreement the churches affirmed the Calvinist theology of the Westminster Confession, as well as both the autonomy of the congregation and its obligation of fellowshiping and consulting with other congregations. As time went on, they formed associations for intercongregational cooperation.

Bishops

The Eastern Orthodox, the Roman Catholic Church, and many Episcopalians hold that it is God's will that the church be governed by the high-ranking pastors who have the office of bishop. But this is not the teaching of Scripture.

In the New Testament the Greek words for bishop (or overseer) and pastor (or elder) are used interchangeably (Acts 20:17, 28; Titus 1:5–7). Every pastor of a congregation is the bishop of that congregation. The Greek word for bishop (episcopos) means "overseer." It is not used anywhere in the Bible to indicate a pastor who is the overseer of other pastors. Such a use of that term describes a feature of church administration that developed in history.

The church was and is free to adopt both the custom and the name of bishops, since they are nowhere forbidden in the New Testament. But Scripture does not allow us to call all this the divinely instituted form of church government. It is no small matter to declare that a servant of the church is not a true pastor, or a full pastor, if he is not appointed to the office by an overseeing bishop. Lutherans rightly object to this opinion.

In the beginning these congregations taught and practiced discipline according to their commitment to Calvinism. They followed the principle of the local church's freedom in the use of creeds. As a result, they could not deal with the rise and spread of liberal theology among them. Doctrinal toleration and indifference have become the dominant attitude in this group, although there has been much conflict in it over Unitarianism, biblical criticism, and many other aberrations.

Through merger Congregationalists have become part of the United Church of Christ.

Henry VIII

Episcopalianism

When King Henry VIII declared the English church to be independent of the Pope (1534), he established the monarch as head of the church. At the first its teaching was his own Roman Catholic doctrine (without the papacy). Later it adopted some of the theology of Lutheranism and Calvinism. All the bodies that eventually formed throughout the world are called *Anglican,* from the Latin word for England. Some of these, such as the Church of England and the Episcopal Church in the United States, belong to an alliance known as the Anglican Communion. They meet every 10 years in the Lambeth Conference.

Statements of the Episcopalian Heritage

The 39 Articles of Faith were formulated in 1563, under Queen Elizabeth I. They provide a minimal basis for a comprehensive national church. It was designed to include differing parties and viewpoints, as long as extremes were avoided. The language of the Articles allowed differing interpretations by those who subscribed.

The 39 Articles are used with varying degrees of strictness by the different Anglican bodies. Some, like the largest Episcopalian church in the United States, do not require subscription at all. The Church of England still requires subscription, but allows qualified subscription. The more conservative bodies tend to take the 39 Articles more seriously.

The Lambeth Quadrilateral shows the policy of comprehensiveness. This statement was adopted and has been used by the Lambeth Conference since 1888. It affirms the fourfold basis of unity that Anglicans ask for, both for unity within their own communion and for fellowship between Anglicans and other denominations:

1. The Scriptures as the rule of faith
2. The Apostles' and Nicene Creeds
3. The sacraments of Baptism and the Lord's Supper
4. Episcopal church government Episcopalians allow a wide difference of opinion on all four points.

Church Government

The name *Episcopalian* indicates the church's form of church government—by bishops (from *episcopos,* the Greek word for bishop). Some Episcopalians hold that government by bishops belongs to the essence of the Christian church; without bishops, there is no church, but simply Christians who are not yet incorporated into the church. Others assert that episcopalian government is the most beneficial for the church, but not essential to the church's being. They understand point 4 of the Lambeth Quadrilateral to be simply an insistence that episcopal government is to be preferred. Still others hold that Christians without bishops are truly members of the church, but the church structure intended by the Lord does not fully exist among them.

The "Umbrella Church"

The compromising, moderating spirit of the 39 Articles has been expanded more and more. The church today has an "umbrella" that covers many: those who follow very elaborate liturgical practices and those who place little importance on liturgical practices; those who stress government by bishops and those who do not; evangelical conservatives and radical liberals. We see a general lack of theological direction among Anglican churches.

Because the 39 Articles are most readily understood as a statement of Calvinist teaching, the Episcopalian church is commonly labeled a Calvinistic church. But Arminians, Lutherans, Roman Catholics, and others have influenced its teaching and life. Some have identified three tendencies in Episcopalianism: *Low Church* (holding Protestant beliefs in various forms), *High Church* (stressing views of government, church, sacraments, and ritual much like those of Roman Catholicism), and *Broad* (or tolerant) *Church*.

A number of smaller bodies have formed in protest against the dominant liberal tendencies in the Anglican churches, notably the ordination of women priests. These have begun to organize a counterpart conservative alliance, sometimes called the Traditional Anglican Communion.

▼
Something to Think About

1. Describe the Presbyterians' attitude toward their doctrinal heritage.

2. Compare Calvinist and Lutheran teachings on saving grace.

3. Why do Lutherans disagree with the doctrine of limited atonement?

4. What is "immediate grace"? What are some problems with that concept?

5. Contrast Lutheran and Calvinist teachings about the Lord's Supper. How is this related to the way each thinks of Jesus Christ?

6. Explain the three widely held views of church government: *Episcopalian, Presbyterian,* and *Congregationalist*. Why is it important to know how to judge ideas about church government?

7. How does the Calvinistic concept of the Law as a means of grace rob a person of the peace God gives us through the Gospel?

8. Explain the difficulties congregationalist churches have in dealing with false doctrine in their midst.

9. Describe the place of the 39 Articles in the Episcopalian heritage.

10. Some say there are three tendencies in the Episcopalian Church—High Church, Low Church, and Broad Church. Which of these, do you think, is more like Lutheranism?

5
Arminian Churches

These churches have continued in some form the synergistic theology (that we somehow cooperate with God in our salvation) of Jacob (James) Arminius (1560–1609), a professor of theology at the University of Leyden (in the Netherlands). The ministers trained under him caused widespread controversy as they taught his doctrines. They expressed these doctrines in a statement called the "Remonstrance" (Protest) against traditional Calvinism. These were repudiated by the Synod of Dort, convened in the Netherlands (1618–19).

The Arminian "Remonstrance" stated these ideas:

> While fallen humanity is seriously corrupted in its spiritual capacities, human will still has some freedom and ability to play a role in regeneration.

> There is no predestination except one conditioned on God's foreknowledge of man's use of free will to believe.

> The Savior died for all, and all can benefit by His atonement.

> The free will of man can both resist and reject God's grace.

> Grace can be lost.

These views have influenced many within the Calvinistic, Episcopalian, and Baptist bodies. They also became the position of numerous bodies formed in later times, notably the Methodists.

The Methodists

The Methodist heritage began with John Wesley, the 17th-century revivalist in England. He called the people out of the moral and spiritual laxity of the time to the faith and holiness of Christian life. His followers were called Methodists because of their concentration on methods and rules for holy living.

Under Wesley's leadership societies were formed in the Church of England. These eventually became independent bodies in Great Britain and throughout the world. The largest in America is the United Methodist Church.

John Wesley

Statements of the Methodist Heritage

The major expressions of the Methodist approach were the Articles of Religion (an adapted version of the Anglican 39 Articles), the Rules of the Methodist Church, and a collection of Wesley's sermons.

Methodists have always shown a great deal of toleration of differences. In this they follow Wesley himself. He held that Christians should believe basic biblical truth, like verbal inspiration or the Incarnation, but he did not care to spend much time disputing the way people express these truths. Nor did he require precise agreement in theology.

To some extent Wesley insisted on the importance of Christian tradition, but he was tolerant of doctrinal looseness and was not bothered much by diversity of teaching. He said, "As to all opinions which do not strike at the root of Christianity, we think and let think" ("The Character of a Methodist," *The Works of the Rev. John Wesley, M.A.,* VIII, 340) and "I believe the merciful God regards the lives and tempers of men more than their ideas" (*The Sermons of the Rev. John Wesley, M.A.,* II, 485; from J. Mudge, *Heart Religion as Described by John Wesley,* p. 10). These statements reflect the characteristic Methodist approach to use of confessional statements. Some, especially in the United Methodist Church, are doctrinally permissive even in what they consider to be the basics of Christian teaching.

Grace and Free Will

Like Wesley, Methodists hold the views of Arminius listed earlier. They agree with his version of the Arminian concept of free will in conversion: Fallen nature has actually lost it, but God has restored this freedom in all human beings so that they might use it in cooperating in their conversion. (But according to the Bible, regeneration is solely the work and gift of God, 2 Cor. 4:6; Eph. 2:1, 5.)

Methodists believe that forgiveness of sins is freely given by God's grace in Christ. But they also accept the general Arminian idea that Jesus' works of obedience to God are not credited to those who believe in Him. They teach that Christians are enabled by sanctification to do their own holy works, which qualify them for eternal life. (But the fact is that the good works of Christians, even the best of them, are never perfect and acceptable in themselves—Is. 64:6; Phil. 3:9. Christ's perfect obedience must be credited to us—Rom. 5:19.)

The Means of Grace

Methodists, like other Arminians, are similar to the Calvinists in their understanding of means of grace. They use the term but understand it to refer to divinely appointed activities in which people receive help from God (not instruments by which forgiveness is given). Some Methodists, like Wesley himself, do recognize baptismal regeneration of infants.

Full Salvation

Wesley often used this term to refer to the full experience of salvation that a Christian is to have. It includes not only assurance of salvation through faith in Christ, but also what Wesley called *Christian perfection* and *entire sanctification*. This is the highest state of grace, in which Christians become so sanctified that they no longer commit acts of sin. (But God says otherwise—1 John 1:7–8.)

Church Government

Even though Methodists see the office of bishop as a human custom, bishops exercise a great deal of power over their congregations. Most Methodist churches have episcopal polity, but some smaller bodies function without a system of bishops.

The Salvation Army

The Salvation Army began as a movement organized by the Methodist evangelist William Booth (1829–1912) to carry on his work in the slums of East London and later in other parts of England and overseas. The name indicates the military pattern adopted for carrying on "campaigns" against unbelief and sin. Mission stations are called "corps." Ministers are "officers" with uniforms (Booth was the "general" of the army). Members are "soldiers" who sign a doctrinal summary called "The Articles of War."

From the time of Booth the Salvation Army has followed the principle that spiritual work and social work must go hand in hand. He said that a hungry man must be fed before he will hunger for God. The Army, or the Salvationists (as they are often called), is well known and respected for its social-welfare program.

The Salvation Army's theology has Arminian and Methodist emphases. Its central theme is holiness of life. While fallen humanity is deeply corrupt, it does not lack the willpower to choose to accept the salvation that God offers because of Jesus Christ. A Christian can attain sinless perfection.

After the Army's "campaign" began in America in 1880, efforts were made to establish an independent American Salvationist organization. This caused a division in the Army and led to the formation of two groups, the American Rescue Workers and the Volunteers of America.

The organization, work, and theology of all these bodies are similar. An important difference has to do with Baptism and the Lord's Supper. The Salvation Army considers these sacraments unnecessary. They were merely symbolic ceremonies in the early church, not instituted as permanent rites. Only the truths they symbolize are necessary. In contrast, the American Rescue Workers, like the Methodists, see Baptism and the Lord's Supper as duly appointed acts for the Christian church. The Volunteers of America administer them to those who desire them.

The Holiness Movement and the Perfectionist Churches

The holiness movement developed in the 19th century among people who felt that church leaders did not place enough stress on holiness in the Christian life. Many formed new bodies to advocate Wesley's doctrine of Christian perfection.

The largest of these perfectionist bodies is the Church of the Nazarene. Nazarenes share Wesley's views about Christ's death for all, humanity's role in their conversion, and the complete sanctification of believers so that they stop sinning. Also, Nazarenes believe that people experience the baptism with the Holy Spirit following conversion. This baptism works complete sanctification by rooting all sin from the heart. They expect a premillennial return of Christ, and many believe that healing of sickness through faith is guaranteed by Jesus' atonement.

The "Full Gospel" of the Pentecostal Churches

The second phase of the Holiness Movement was Pentecostalism. Around 1900 some Holiness preachers in America were calling for an emotional experience of the Spirit in addition to entire sanctification. They taught that the apostles' experience at Pentecost is necessary for the full Christian life.

Many bodies were formed. These include the Assemblies of God (the largest in this country and in the world), the Church of the Foursquare Gospel, the Church of God (Cleveland, Tenn.), and the Church of God in Christ.

All these churches claim that they have restored the "full gospel"—the true list of essential blessings that the believer should expect. It is a fourfold message about Christ:

> Christ the Savior
> Christ the Sanctifier
> Christ the Healer
> Christ the Coming King

As Sanctifier, Christ baptizes with His Spirit to endow with power for life and service. Some, but not all, Pentecostals say that this baptism works entire sanctification from sin. All say that the sign of speaking with tongues is the necessary initial sign that one truly has this baptism and this full possession of the Spirit.

Pentecostals hold that healing now in this life is a privilege made available to Christians by Christ's atonement. It can be received by faith just as surely as the forgiveness of sins which He earned for us. Pentecostals claim that it is not God's will that anyone should be unhealthy, and so He has provided for healing. Sick Christians should simply lay claim to what is promised here. All believers can obtain it for themselves if their faith is strong enough.

The gift of healing is an ability given to some to convey this benefit of the atonement to others by prayer, and also by commanding disease to come out of the sick body. When healers fail, or when a healed person relapses soon after the healing, the person is said not to have strong enough faith.

The coming king will establish His kingdom for a thousand years. Pentecostals accept the premillennialist interpretation of Revelation 20. The millennium is expected to be the climax of the activity of Christ and His Spirit. They regard the tongues, healing, and other phenomena emphasized by their movement as signs of the Second Advent.

Pentecostals are dispensationalists in that they view the church age (or dispensation) and salvation by grace through faith in Christ as a temporary arrangement rather than as God's plan of salvation from the beginning. They think the church age will come to an end and a millennium will follow. During the millennium God may provide means of salvation other than Word and Sacrament in the church.

▼
Something to Think About

1. Who was Arminius?
2. Contrast the Calvinist doctrines summarized by the letters TULIP with the opposite Arminian doctrines. Which of all these points agree with Scripture?
3. What approach to the use of confessional statements comes from John Wesley?
4. What did John Wesley teach about the freedom of the will?
5. Contrast Wesley's view of imputed righteousness with biblical teaching.
6. What is "entire sanctification"? Why can we not support this teaching?
7. Why do we say the Salvation Army belongs to the Arminian family of churches?
8. Compare Methodist and Salvation Army teachings about Baptism and the Lord's Supper. Show the biblical basis for insisting that we continue to use these sacraments.
9. Why are the Pentecostal churches called by this name?
10. What is meant by "the Full Gospel"? How does Scripture disagree with that concept?
11. Suppose a Pentecostal says, "You have not been baptized with the Holy Spirit." What is he or she talking about? How do you respond?
12. Perhaps a friend is very ill. A well-meaning co-worker or neighbor advises that your friend should pray harder and have a stronger faith. Then healing will result. What is wrong with that advice? Where is the comfort in that advice?
13. The Bible teaches that God hears and answers our prayers. What does that really mean? How do you answer someone who has prayed for healing or deliverance, but the illness or trouble continues?
14. What claims are made by Pentecostals about *tongues*? Why can we not support those claims?

6

Alternatives to Infant Baptism

Most Protestant churches view Holy Baptism as no more than a sign of the work of grace and of God's Spirit in a person's heart. Some even teach that it is simply a believer's symbolic profession of faith. They therefore conclude that infants should not be baptized, since they are not capable of making such a conscious profession.

The Mennonites

The Mennonite Church and related bodies carry on the teaching of the Anabaptists of the 16th century. They were organized under the leadership of Menno Simons, a contemporary of Luther. Several groups exist, and some are stricter than others. Some—the Amish—are named after the 17th-century leader J. Amman. They adhere to his teaching that in church discipline the excommunicated should be shunned even in social relationships.

Statements of the Mennonite Heritage

Mennonites have written a number of statements of doctrine. The Dordrecht Confession (1632) is most widely used. All these statements are anticreedal, not requiring their pastors and churches to subscribe to them. Nevertheless, Mennonites use and value statements of doctrine for purposes of educating their own members and clarifying their theology.

Life in the Spirit

Mennonites emphasize a holy life centered in experience of the Holy Spirit. Many times Anabaptists and Mennonites have claimed to be guided by revelations, dreams, and impulses they have received from the Spirit. For example, at the very beginning of the movement, Konrad Grebel felt guided to start a brotherhood of rebaptized people (Anabaptists). That is, he spread the doctrine that infant baptism is invalid. A Mennonite college in Waterloo, Ontario, is named after Grebel.

The emphasis on experience has a natural connection with the refusal to baptize infants and also with a synergistic conception of free will. It is taught that we have the ability to hear the good offered by God and to admit or reject it.

This emphasis shows itself in Mennonite doctrine of justification. The Dordrecht Confession, Article IV, does teach that justification is made possible by the sacrifice of Jesus. But Article V shows that faith and works are mixed together in this teaching.

The heading of Article V reads: "Of the Law of Christ, Which Is the Holy Gospel." This article contains the Mennonite teaching that we are acceptable to God through our works: "All men without distinction, if they are obedient, through faith, follow, fulfill and live according to the precepts of the same, are His children and rightful heirs." Justification is based on Christ-in-us (our holy life) rather than Christ-for-us (His righteousness credited as ours by free grace—which is the theology of Scripture).

Nonconformity

Passages like Rom. 12:2, which tell Christians not to be conformed to this world, are important to Mennonites. They understand these words to teach that we have a Christian duty to use only what is necessary. This nonuse of worldly things is more faithful to the New Testament, they say, than other ways of living. Mennonites differ in applying the principle of nonconformity. Some use buggies in place of autos and do not use phones or electricity. These are called "hook-and-eye Mennonites," so called because they don't use buttons. Traditional Mennonite clothes are "plain dress," simple and somber in hue, to express rejection of vanity and frivolity. Other Mennonites are less strict.

Mennonites also hold that Christ forbids His people to participate in the world's activities of government and warfare.

The Quakers

The various groups of Quakers, or the Society of Friends, are similar in many respects to the Mennonites. They, too, emphasize the experience of the Spirit, direct illuminations from God, cooperation with God in obtaining salvation, refusal to use statements of their heritage as pledges for their leaders, and opposition to military service.

The fellowship of the Friends began under George Fox in the 17th century. He emphasized reliance on the direct guidance of the Spirit (the "Inner Light"). Friends have applied this in numerous ways in their beliefs. They see Holy Scripture as a record of the Inner Light experiences of men of old. It is secondary, they say, to one's own direct consciousness of the Inner Light. Quakers view Scripture as a useful guide, but they differ as to how reliable it is.

Friends teach that people take part in their conversion and justification by working together with the Inner Light and the Holy Spirit. Christians are to live by the guidance and power of this inner working. The Friends say that the Inner Light experience demonstrates the equality of all human beings, since all have access to it.

The worship of the most traditional Quakers is the "silent meeting" of communion with the Spirit, without sermon, hymn, or liturgy. Some of the early Friends experienced quaking and trembling in their meetings. The name *Quaker* came from contemporary society's perception of what was happening at meetings of the Society of Friends.

Baptism, Quakers teach, is unnecessary not only for infants, but even for adults. Like the Salvation Army, the Friends regard both it and the Lord's Supper as outdated symbols of the Spirit-filled life of faith. They teach that Jesus did not institute them to be permanent and indispensable ceremonies of Christianity. Rather, they are like object lessons, similar to the foot washing in John 13:1–12.

Furthermore, the service of pastors is not necessary in the church, unless one has a call to it through the Inner Light. The groups that are closer to Christian orthodoxy, the Friends United Meeting and Evangelical Friends, tend to emphasize and employ the use of pastors in the life of the church more than other Quakers.

The Baptists

The first Baptist churches originated among the English Separatists (Congregationalists) at the beginning of the 17th century. They have organized into many separate groups, and the Southern Baptists have become the largest of all Protestant denominations. Other large organizations are the various black national Baptist bodies and the American Baptist Churches in the U.S.A.

Statements of the Baptist Heritage

Baptists declare liberty of conscience to be their central emphasis. They claim freedom from human authority in all religious matters. This freedom extends to the way believers in Christ exercise their spiritual lives.

While Baptists have never required confessional subscription of their pastors, they have

Font or River?

Baptists argue that a Baptism not done by immersion is not a true Baptism. That is to say, if the water is sprinkled or poured at a Baptism font in a church, no Baptism takes place. The one being baptized must be submerged in water. Baptism may take place in a church if the church uses a container, such as a tank or even a very large font, with capacity for enough water to do in church what could be done in a river.

However, the New Testament does not require this mode. Therefore Christians are free to use it or not use it as they wish. Typically, Baptists reply to this statement by saying that the requirement is contained in the Greek word that is used in the New Testament for baptize (baptizo). This word, they say, means "immerse." However, that same word is sometimes used to mean simply wash or apply water. This is clear in certain Bible passages:

In Luke 11:38 the Greek word is used to describe the Jewish handwashing ceremony, which was simply done by pouring, not by immersion.

Heb. 9:10 uses a form of the Greek word to describe Old Testament washings. These did not always involve submersion in water. For instance, one who was defiled by touching a dead body was sprinkled (Num. 19:13).

Lutherans do not disagree with Baptists that the use of water in Baptism is meant to impress upon us that we are immersed in God's redemptive work in Christ. But we believe that God has promised to use Baptism as an instrument to bring about this benefit. The amount of water used to make this impression does not really matter. For example, Luther in his Large Catechism tells how in Baptism

"the body has water poured over it" (Baptism, 45). Later he describes what is signified by the water:

Finally, we must know what Baptism signifies and why God ordained just this sign and external observance for the sacrament by which we are first received into the Christian church. This act or observance consists in being dipped into the water, which covers us completely, and being drawn out again. These two parts, being dipped under the water and emerging from it, indicate the power and effect of Baptism, which is simply the slaying of the old Adam and the resurrection of the new man, both of which actions must continue in us our whole life long. Thus a Christian life is nothing else than a daily Baptism once begun and ever continued. (64–65; Tappert, pp. 444–45)

often written and used statements of doctrine for educational and other purposes. These include the New Hampshire Confession, the Southern Baptist Faith and Message Statement, and the Philadelphia Confession.

A Baptist congregation usually has a statement of faith and a covenant pledge with which members are asked to agree. But congregations commonly tolerate a loose interpretation and qualified acceptance of these statements.

Baptists are zealous advocates of religious liberty, which is an obvious political application of liberty of conscience. The state must not impose anything on the individual in matters of conscience.

Believer's Immersion

Baptists hold that believer's immersion is the only proper form of Baptism. It is to be a believer's Baptism, used by a believer to express the person's faith symbolically. Thus if one was an unbeliever at the time, it was an invalid Baptism.

No infant can be a believer. Infant Baptism is useless, immoral, and unnecessary (since Baptism is necessary only for those who understand their obligation).

The complete covering with water symbolizes burial with Christ. The Baptists see both Baptism and the Lord's Supper simply as symbols, but as necessary symbols.

Other Beliefs of Baptists

Great diversity exists among Baptists. Some hold traditional Calvinist views about grace and conversion. Others adhere to Arminian ideas about free will in conversion. Often they forbid things that God does not. For example, some insist upon teetotalism, the view that God demands total abstinence from alcohol.

Various other religious bodies also reject infant Baptism. These include the Disciples of Christ, many holiness bodies, millennialist groups, and cultic groups. These are discussed in other chapters.

Something to Think About

1. Explain the difference between the biblical teaching of justification based on Christ-for-us and the Mennonite concept of justification based on Christ-in-us.

2. Evaluate the Mennonite teachings of pacifism and conformity.

3. Explain how the Inner Light idea is important to Quakers. In what way does this concept of God-given light contain both truth and error?

4. What do the Friends lose by not using the sacraments?

5. How would you reply to a Baptist friend who tells you, "We don't make our pastors subscribe to human documents, as you Lutherans do, because we believe their liberty of conscience should be recognized."

6. How is an emphasis on experience in the heart related to (a) a synergistic concept of free will? (b) a refusal to baptize infants?

7. Why do Lutherans defend the practice of infant Baptism?

8. How does your Baptism affect your life?

9. What does Scripture teach about immersion?

10. Luther encouraged people to say, "I am baptized," not "I was baptized." Why do you think he made that distinction?

11. What does Scripture teach about total abstinence from alcohol?

7

Movements in the Churches

Liberalism

The advocates of religious liberalism emphasize freedom from tradition and authority. They claim to apply religious beliefs to modern scientific conceptions and modern thought, and also to adjust and conform the beliefs accordingly. Human reason becomes master in theology. Proponents make extensive use of historical criticism, which treats the Bible like any other book and does not recognize that, as God's Word, it is free from error and self-contradiction. (But Scripture warns against the tendency of reason to lord it over revelation. See 1 Cor. 1:25; 2:4, 5, 14; 2 Cor. 10:5; Rom. 8:7; and Col. 2:8.)

Religious liberals vary in their disagreement with the Christian teachings of historic denominations. They differ widely as to which doctrines they attack. Sometimes they discard doctrines, and sometimes they pay lip service to a doctrine while "reinterpreting" it.

Some groups, like the Unitarians, have been liberal in their outlook from the outset. Others at one time showed great respect for the inspired Word of truth—even when they did not rightly understand and accept all the doctrines in it—but have been influenced by liberal trends. This deplorable condition has come to pass in almost all major church bodies, Roman Catholic and Protestant. It has caused severe conflict between the liberals and those who want to hold firm to the "ancient paths" (Jer. 6:16).

The controversies have involved such matters as the reliability of Holy Scripture in all that it states, the concept of propositional revelation (communication of God-given words and statements), the Holy Trinity, the deity of Christ, His virgin birth, His vicarious satisfaction, the bodily resurrection of Christ or of anyone else, justification by being credited with Christ's righteousness, the creation of the world in six days, and the unalterable moral standards of God's Law.

Conservatives who oppose liberal trends are often called Evangelicals. This broad term refers in general to the intention to preach and defend the truths of the Gospel. It describes people who carry out this intention in different ways. Some are called Fundamentalists, after the term used in a Baptist church paper in 1921 to describe those who insisted upon the confession of a certain number of fundamental Christian teachings. Other conservative Evangelicals emphasize free will and are more open to modern scholarly ideas and social concerns than are the Fundamentalists.

Many liberals claim loyalty to their denominations' heritage. The historic doctrinal differences between denominations remain for them. At the same time, liberalism creates an erosion of loyalty to denominations. This creates new concerns and complications for those who seek the unity of the church on the basis of doctrinal agreement.

Liberalism and the reactions to it cut across denominational lines. In many cases the doctrinal differences within a denomination are greater than those that separate it from other denominations.

Unionism

Unionism is church union, fellowship, or joint worship and church work without thorough doctrinal agreement. Ecumenists often base their unionism on the idea that the body of Christ is a visible organization. Because Scripture calls the body of Christ "one," some say that it does not exist, or fully exist, in modern divided Christendom. Or they say that it is found in a form without external organizational unity (which they say is a divinely instituted and essential structural feature).

Such thinking can lead to a demand for union of visible church bodies without theological agreement. Persons may insist on the union of theologically conflicting visible church bodies, basing the union on the lowest common denominator. This was the meaning of a famous statement made in 1937 by Archbishop William Temple. He told an interdenomina-

tional assembly (which later grew into the World Council of Churches), "I believe in the holy catholic church—and sincerely regret that it does not at present exist!" The oneness of the body of Christ is to be brought about by the negotiations of the churches. We are told that we have a duty to do so, because of Jesus' prayer "that they may be one" (John 17:22).

The same sort of idea was put forth in the Evanston Report of the World Council of Churches (1954), which stated that the body of Christ is the sum or totality of the visible churches. Again, the body of Christ is described as a divided body that must yet be unified.

The Lutheran Church—Missouri Synod is committed to true ecumenism and the external expression of church unity in a responsible way.

Eph. 4:3 expresses the apostle's teaching that we are to keep the unity of the Spirit in the bond of peace. The bond of peace is the life of peaceful relationships with one another. Christians can bring about or can break this unity. Thus, it is an external expression of unity. In this outward bond or fellowship relation, God does direct us to endeavor to express a unity of the Spirit. Such unity, however, is not brought about by human effort. Rather it is God's creation in the church. Paul describes it as "one body and one Spirit—just as you were called to one hope when you were called—one Lord, one faith, one baptism" (Eph. 4:4–5).

In John 17:22 Jesus prays that the believers may all be one. Unionists misinterpret this as prayer for something that has not yet come about. In fact, God answered this prayer when He created the church, which necessarily always has a unity of all believers in Christ. All believers must have faith in Christ as Savior, and that faith unites them in one body. Divisions exist in the way that this unity is expressed in the many church bodies and their relations with one another, but that unity is a constant.

The efforts to bring about outward expressions of the inner unity of the church must be done in a responsible way, not in a way that supports and continues the teaching of false doctrine. Then "we will no longer be infants,

Union without Unity

Doctrinal differences create walls that separate church people into groups. Many desire to join hands across the walls in a unified organization or in joint performance of the work of the church. They want to unite in spite of doctrinal differences. This is union without unity in doctrine.

But faithful Christians should not work with or give approval to religious leaders who are leading people into unsound doctrine (2 John 9; Rom. 16:17). For example, we support the Baptism of infants, and we work against our convictions if we unite with those who attack infant Baptism. We must avoid whatever hinders us from following the apostle Paul in declaring the whole will of God (Acts 20:27).

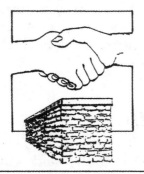

tossed back and forth by the waves, and blown here and there by every wind of teaching" (Eph. 4:14).

Responsible ecumenism must be faithful to the revealed truth and call all others to do likewise. The early church acted in this way (Acts 2:42). And Paul says:

> I appeal to you, brothers, in the name of our Lord Jesus Christ, that all of you agree with one another so that there may be no divisions among you and that you may be perfectly united in mind and thought. (1 Cor. 1:10; see also Rom. 15:5–6)

St. Paul sums up the effect of this united and likeminded testimony to God and His Word in his instruction to avoid those who cause divisions contrary to right doctrine (Rom. 16:17). This is the responsible approach to unity. We must avoid those who, by promoting doctrines contrary to apostolic teaching, cause divisions. We cannot unite with them to do the work of the church, because we can't agree with them on what to teach.

This is the confessional approach of the Lutheran church, which holds to the truth and cannot with good conscience enter into fellowship relations with those who hold false beliefs. We reject denominationalism, the view that the variety of differing teachings of the denominations is good and God-pleasing. This unscriptural view holds that all church doctrines are versions of the same truth and express the same teaching of God's Word.

Lutherans hold that the followers of Christ have a solemn responsibility to remain faithful to His truth and to express disapproval of those who hold false beliefs (Matt. 28:20a; John 8:31–32; 1 Tim. 1:3; 6:3–5; Titus 1:13–14). Therefore Lutherans cannot unite with the defenders of doctrinal errors in a church union that supports and encourages those errors. Lutherans insist:

> We have no intention (since we have no authority to do so) to yield anything of the eternal and unchangeable truth of God for the sake of temporal peace, tranquillity, and outward harmony.... We have a sincere delight in deep love for true harmony and are cordially inclined and determined on our part

to do everything in our power to further the same. We desire such harmony as will not violate God's honor, that will not detract anything from the divine truth of the holy Gospel, that will not give place to the smallest error but will lead the poor sinner to true and sincere repentance, raise him up through faith, strengthen him in his new obedience, and thus justify and save him for ever through the sole merit of Christ, and so forth. (Formula of Concord XI; Tappert, p. 632)

Union Churches

Some churches have been formed according to the principle of unionism.

The Moravian Motto

> *In essentials unity, in nonessentials liberty, in all things charity.*

> *This is the motto of the Moravian Church. The Moravian Book of Order states the eight essentials of the Gospel for which they ask agreement. Disagreement is then allowed in other points, including the ways the essentials are taught.*

The Moravian Church

This body was formed by the followers of John Huss in Bohemia and Moravia in 1457. At that time it declared that a godly life is more important than full agreement in doctrinal formulations. This principle has always been characteristic of the Moravians.

After almost being exterminated, this body was reorganized in the 18th century in the colony of Herrnhut ("the Lord's protection"), on the estate of Count Zinzendorf in Saxony. This was a union of the Hussites with Lutherans and Calvinists. Herrnhut is now the center of worldwide Moravianism. The church is known for its beautiful liturgy, rich hymnody, and zeal for mission work, which brought it to the United States.

The Christian Churches

A movement in the early 19th century attempted to bring about church unity through the restoration of New Testament Christianity. Supporters of this movement—called "Restorationists" and "Christians"—tried to cut through the maze of what they considered to be unwarranted denominationalism. Contrary to their intentions, their movement produced new denominations to separate Christians.

Some of the congregations formed a body known as the Christian Church or the General Convention of the Christian Church. This developed from a union of restorationist movements in North Carolina, New England, and Kentucky. This group desired complete doctrinal freedom and release from their former denominational loyalties. They allowed all individual interpretations of Scripture and required only "Christian character" as a measure of membership. An outspoken Unitarianism was the dominant position, and they were commonly known as Unitarian Baptists. The body eventually became part of the United Church of Christ.

The followers of Alexander Campbell formed another "Christian" group, known to this day as the Disciples of Christ. They claim to be restoring the faith, spirit, and practice of Christ and the apostles, as found in the New Testament. That is, they say, they are restoring the simple Gospel, basic Christianity, and do not add human requirements for church membership; all confessions of faith are just human requirements.

The Disciples of Christ say they are restoring the true church, as it was intended to be. They claim that the original Christian church was unified because it did not require anything for membership beyond profession of faith in Jesus Christ and obedience to Him. They teach that passages like "believe in the Lord Jesus, and you will be saved" (Acts 16:31) mean that the church was never concerned about full unity in doctrine.

Barton Stone and Thomas and Alexander Campbell led the 19th-century movement that resulted in the formation of the Disciples of Christ. These men insisted that nothing should be made an article of faith or a requirement for church membership or communion fellowship except that which is expressly taught by Scripture. They claimed that doctrines like the Holy Trinity, the deity of Christ, and vicarious satisfaction are not expressly taught by Scripture because these words or expressions are not found in the biblical text.

Stone and the Campbells taught that the church must tolerate differences in doctrine over all these matters as long as church members professes faith in Christ and are willing to affirm the words of the Bible. They can have whatever opinions they choose about what the words mean (e.g., what it means to say that Christ is the Son of God). So, for example, a writer in the official organ of the Disciples of Christ could accurately say, "I stand with a long line of Disciples who believe that Jesus, the Christ, is the Son of God, but not God" (*The Christian*, Nov. 26, 1961). Deductions from the words of the Bible, even if they are correct, can never be made binding on the consciences of Christians. Therefore creeds can never be used as a test of fitness for membership or a norm for church discipline.

The motto of the Campbellite churches is

No creed but Christ,
No Book but the Bible,
No Name but the Divine
In essentials unity, in opinions liberty, in
all things charity.

This approach led to wide diversity of religious opinions and doctrines. However, the Campbellites differ among themselves as to how far they should go in applying this principle of toleration. The Disciples of Christ allow the most diversity and widest toleration. The splinter groups are comparatively more conservative. They teach that obedience to Christ must include certain doctrines, like the Trinity and the deity of Christ; these should be regarded as necessary teachings of the Bible, even if the exact words are not found in the text, because the concepts are there. But even the splinter groups do not call for full unity of doctrine.

The Campbellites don't distinguish between the invisible church of all believers and the visible church. To them the Christian church is the visible organization that they have restored according to the New Testament pattern of doing things. Christians either belong to that organization or they are outside the church.

The Campbellites also hold that the New Testament contains the blueprint for the organization, government, and practices that must be followed in the Christian church. They teach that the New Testament regulates the ceremony and organization of the church just as the Law of Moses regulated the Old Testament community. There can be disunity in doctrine, but there must be unity in practice.

The Campbells claimed that the blueprint for the church was not being fully followed in all its details by any Christian group at the beginning of the 19th century. Therefore the Christian church did not exist in its full, authentic form. That is, none of the existing churches was the same as the New Testament church, because they had different names, a different organization, different terms of membership, and different practices than what the New Testament church used. None of them was a continuation of the church founded by Christ. The Campbells were restoring that church.

The blueprint requires, among other things, a congregational church structure, adult believers' immersion, the performance of Baptism and the Lord's Supper as acts of obedience, the rejection of creeds, and the principle of confessional compromise (fellowship on the basis of the least common denominator). It also calls for the use of a nondenominational name, that is, one of the names by which believers called themselves in the New Testament. Thus, the original group wished to be known as the Disciples of Christ or as Christians. The splinter groups have called themselves the Christian churches or the Churches of Christ.

Campbellites hold that the blueprint also requires that the Lord's Supper be celebrated every Sunday. They base this on their flawed interpretation of Acts 20:7, "On the first day of the week we [the disciples] came together to break bread." In fact, this verse reports what the Christians in Troas did. The Campbellites interpret it to be a norm for all Christians to follow.

In addition, differences and divisions have arisen among the Campbellites over whether things not commanded in the New Testament are contrary to the New Testament blueprint for the church. Some have maintained that they are. Therefore the Campbellites have split up over such issues as whether organs and other instruments should be used in worship; whether pastors should be called "Reverend"; and whether certain other structures may exist—structures such as congregational mission societies or Sunday schools, national church organizations with boards and officers, and ministerial associations.

Scripture rejects Restorationist ideas about diversity in doctrine. St. Paul says in 1 Cor. 1:10, "I appeal to you, brothers, in the name of our Lord Jesus Christ, that all of you agree with one another so that there may be no divisions among you and that you may be perfectly united in mind and thought." We do not fulfill this by simply requiring all members to make a very general statement such as, "Jesus is the Son of God," while allowing total disagreement over what it means.

None of these Campbellites believe that original sin is inherited at birth, although they believe that all people become sinners after they grow old enough to become accountable for their actions. This belief denies any need for infant Baptism.

Still, the Campbellites have a long-standing controversy with the Baptists. Both groups teach that Baptism is a symbolic act of immersion by which believers express their faith and repentance. Baptists teach that at the time of Baptism a person must be regenerated; if not, the Baptism is not valid. But the Campbellites teach that people are never regenerated at the time of Baptism; Baptism is an act of obedience that fulfills the requirements of what a person must do to obtain regeneration; it is not a work of God that brings about regeneration. Thus, they teach, a believer who never gets an immersion has failed to perform a necessary act of obedience and is not reborn. The strictest Campbellites hold that such a person cannot be saved. But others say that the person is justified and forgiven in his or her heart, even if not in fact.

Independent Churches

Many congregations call themselves "independent" to indicate partial or total independence of control by any denominational or ecclesiastical organization. Some use a denominational name but work without denominational supervision. Others are community churches—local churches that accept members from any Protestant denomination and have a broad doctrinal basis. Still others are congregations formed from the union of congregations having different denominational backgrounds. A variation on this are the federated churches—two or more congregations of different denominations that make use of a common pastor and program but retain separate identity and denominational affiliation.

The term "community church" is often used for all of these types of congregations. A number of them belong to the Council of Community Churches, formed in 1946. This fellowship for cooperation uses the motto, "We agree to differ, resolve to love, unite to serve."

Other independents repudiate denominational affiliation and separation but hold that a certain amount of doctrinal agreement is necessary for cooperation between congregations. They hold a Fundamentalist viewpoint. The main association formed by them is the Independent Fundamental Churches of America.

The United Church of Canada

The Canadian Methodists, Congregationalists, and some Presbyterians merged in 1925 to form the United Church of Canada. Some other bodies have joined since that time. The statements of faith adopted by this organization allow for differing denominational teachings and interpretation according to either conservative or liberal views.

The United Church of Christ

The United Church of Christ (UCC) was formed by mergers of the Congregationalist Church, the Christian Church (General Convention of the Christian Church), the Reformed Church in the U.S., and the Evangelical Synod of North America. The Congregationalists and the Christians merged in 1931. The Reformed Church in the U.S. and the Evangelical Synod joined in 1934 to form the Evangelical and Reformed Church. The resulting two groups united with each other in 1957.

None of these mergers were based on confessional unity. All of the bodies were characterized by a growing indifference about questions of doctrine.

The old Congregational churches were at one time strongly Calvinistic in doctrine. Their church was formed in the 17th century by the Puritans, who had wanted to purify the Church of England, and who came to America to found the Massachusetts Bay Colony, and the Separatists, who left the Church of England and were the Pilgrims of the Plymouth Colony. They all adopted the church structure of Congregationalism, in the form that stressed the independence of each congregation.

This structure gradually led to the same kind of problems that it has led to among the Baptists. That is, as long as the Calvinist creeds were important to these congregations, they took them seriously; at that time there was concern about doctrinal integrity and cooperation among the Congregationalists to work for doctrinal discipline according to Calvinist views. But there was no written commitment to common confessional standards and no requirement of a confessional bond between congregations. In time the theology degenerated into rationalism and liberalism. The denomination could not prevent this, because each congregation was free to adopt any theology desired by it and its pastor.

The General Convention of the Christian Church, or Unitarian Baptists, was described in a previous section.

The Evangelical and Reformed Church was a unionistic church that did not think the differences between Lutherans and Calvinists were important enough to be divisive.

The UCC has no definite doctrinal position. In 1959 it adopted a Statement of Faith, which is deliberately so vague in its formulations that it will hardly offend anyone, Trinitarian or Unitarian, Lutheran or Calvinist. The statement does not mention the return of Christ. This is deliberate, because many in the UCC are not convinced that He will return. They think the Kingdom will be ushered in by the Christians' actions of love. The Statement is not a denominational creed, but is called "a testimony rather than a test of faith." It is not binding upon any congregation or pastor.

The UCC contains both conservatives and liberals. The conservatives have formed organizations like United Church People for Biblical Witness. But the conservatives do not get much support or encouragement from their denominational leaders or church publications and are vastly outnumbered by liberals.

The UCC may be the most liberal of all major denominations. Their body includes theologians who freely question everything stated in the Bible, including whether God is omnipotent and omniscient and whether Jesus Christ is God. UCC leaders have made it clear that their body does not wish to be a confessional church in the sense of a body that spells out its beliefs. But then they say: This is the only right way to believe.

Cooperative Agencies

Various agencies have been formed for cooperation across denominational lines. Their constitutions indicate their understanding of themselves and their purposes.

The World Council of Churches (WCC)

The WCC is an international, interconfessional organization formed to facilitate expression of unity in fellowship, service, and mission work. It grew out of movements to promote cooperation between denominations in three areas:

1. Missions (especially in the International Missionary Council)
2. Social and international problems (especially in the Universal Christian Council for Life and Work)
3. Discussion of doctrinal disagreements (especially in the World Conference on Faith and Order)

The WCC was formed in 1948 in New Amsterdam by merging of the Council for Life and Work and the Conference on Faith and Order. The International Missionary Council was formally integrated into the organization at New Delhi in 1961. More than 300 bodies now belong to it.

All member bodies must agree to the statement of the constitution adopted at New Delhi that the WCC is "a fellowship of churches which confess the Lord Jesus Christ as God and Savior according to the Scriptures and therefore seek to fulfill their common calling to the glory of the one God, Father, Son, and Holy Spirit."

This is interpreted in such a way as to serve the purposes of unionism. Several confessions are involved:

> Jesus is God
> Jesus is Savior
> Scripture is the norm for theology
> God is triune

The WCC allows a variety of interpretations for all these points among the member churches and their theologians. Many are orthodox on all points, although they may disagree on many other points of theology. But many others interpret the statement "Jesus is God" to mean merely that Jesus functions in the place of God. While the Unitarian Association has been excluded from membership because of the constitutional requirement, some WCC presidents have espoused Unitarian theology.

The confession of Christ as Savior is diluted by views of universalism and anonymous Christianity, asserting that people can be saved in non-Christian religions. Also, many combine the Gospel with Marxist and other political ideas to show how Christ is Savior of the world.

The widespread use of historical criticism erodes the authority of Scripture as the norm for theology.

Members of the WCC are committed to a fellowship with each other. It is true that it is a limited kind of fellowship. Its assemblies do not claim to speak for all the members in doctrinal matters. Nor must any member recognize any other member in the full and true sense of the word. Yet the constitution speaks of a fellowship, and the WCC engages in church work and conducts worship services. Fellowship exists without thorough doctrinal agreement and is based on minimal and ambiguous requirements.

The National Council of Churches of Christ in the United States (NCC)

This agency was established in 1950 as a successor to the Federal Council of Churches of Christ (founded 1908). It provides for cooperation in Christian life and missions, overseas ministry, Christian education, and social objectives, such as civil rights and support of the public schools. All the larger American churches are members, except the Southern Baptist Convention, The Lutheran Church—Missouri Synod, and the Roman Catholic Church.

According to its constitution, the purpose of the communions of the NCC is "to manifest oneness in Him" (Christ). In practice, this requires members to recognize "oneness" with denominations that publicly tolerate denials of the Trinity or Christ's deity, as well as other false teachings. The constitution requires members to "confess Jesus Christ as Divine Lord and Savior," but does not aim to show oneness in Him by a unified testimony of teaching.

The American Council of Christian Churches (ACCC)

The ACCC was organized in 1941. It is an organization of denominations, congregations, and individuals who vigorously oppose the theological and political liberalism dominating

(then) the Federal Council and (later) the National Council of Churches. No ACCC members were allowed to maintain membership in the NCC. The International Council of Christian Churches, a worldwide extension of the ACCC, is a conservative counterpart to the World Council of Churches.

ACCC projects include Christian education, mass communication, evangelism, and home and foreign missions. The constitutional doctrinal statement calls for maintenance of purity of doctrine, but a doctrinal mixture exists in its membership.

The National Association of Evangelicals for United Action (NAE)

Many conservative church leaders felt that the Federal Council did not represent their views and yet did not agree with all the theological views of the American Council. In 1942 they formed their own ecumenical organization, the NAE. This group carries on the same sort of work as the ACCC but does not require members to separate from the National Council. They often prefer to fight liberalism from within. Its worldwide extension is the World Evangelical Fellowship.

Church of Christ Uniting

The Church of Christ Uniting (formerly Consultation on Church Union) is a negotiating group for a number of American denominations who wish to unite into one church body. The following groups have been discussing this project since 1961:

The Episcopal Church in the USA
The Presbyterian Church (USA)
The United Church of Christ
The Disciples of Christ
The Council of Community Churches
The United Methodist Church
The African Methodist Episcopal Church
The African Methodist Episcopal Zion Church
The Christian Methodist Episcopal Church

These groups have produced statements in which they agree to disagree in doctrine and to refrain from requiring subscription to any confessional document. But failure to agree on matters of organization and practice has prevented them from accomplishing unity.

Confessional Alliances

Various federations have been formed for cooperation within families of denominations. Major groupings include the Baptist World Alliance, the World Methodist Council, the World Alliance of Reformed Churches (including Presbyterian, Reformed, and Congregational churches), and the Anglican Communion. Other alliances, such as the Reformed Ecumenical Synod, have been formed by conservatively inclined bodies who do not wish to federate with their more liberal counterparts.

The Lutheran World Federation has existed since 1948. The Lutheran Church—Missouri Synod and other nonmember bodies object because LWF members are not united in unqualified adherence to the Lutheran Confessions. Yet, according to its constitution "the members of the Lutheran World Federation understand themselves to be in pulpit and altar fellowship with each other." Confessional Lutherans have formed the International Lutheran Conference.

Millennialism

Already during the early years of the Christian church some Christians defended the view that the thousand years' reign with Christ depicted in Rev. 20:6 should be understood as a visible political dominion of the saints at the end of history. This is called the *millennium,* from the Latin words for thousand years. Many people in many religious groups have adopted some form of this view.

General Themes

Millennialism teaches that at the end of time there will be a golden age of prosperity and peace. This will carry out the work of the Messiah predicted in Is. 2:4; 11:6–9; and other Old Testament passages. At that time the redeemed people of God will reign over their enemies. Satan will be bound or restrained in his destructive activity (Rev. 20:2–3). He and his followers will revolt at the end of the millennium and will ultimately be cast into the lake of fire. Then Christ will reign supreme forever.

Postmillennialism is the idea that Christ will return after (*post* in Latin) the millennium has taken place. The Christian church's influence and success will grow in the world to bring about the millennium of righteousness and peace. Premillennialism is the doctrine that He will return before (*pre* in Latin) the Millennium and will institute it Himself. It teaches that there will be a resurrection of the righteous at the beginning of the millennium and another of the wicked when Christ comes again a thousand years later.

Postmillennialism has been a popular view in the past, though not many churches and persons still hold it. Some, like the Seventh-Day Adventists, and even a number of Lutherans, have carried on the premillennial teaching passed down from early church history. Others have altered this teaching by adding dispensational ideas to it. (These will be described in a later section.)

In fact, the messianic kingdom is not a visible, earthly kingdom. Jesus clearly says, "My kingdom is not of this world" (John 18:36). The messianic kingdom does not originate from political and military maneuvers, and it does not operate by means of political power, but by spiritual weapons and the powers of truth (Eph. 6:11–17; 2 Cor. 10:4–5).

Furthermore, a figurative book of visions like Revelation should not be interpreted literally. The meaning of the images must be found by comparing those images with other Scripture passages. For example, the reign with Christ is a picture of the wonderful relationship Christians have with Christ now (Eph. 2:6; 2 Peter 2:9). And the binding of Satan is the deliverance from his power brought about by the Savior (Heb. 2:14–15; Acts 26:18; Col. 1:13–14).

We especially take notice that the resurrection of the believers cannot take place a thousand years before that of the unbelievers on the Last Day, because Jesus says in John 6:39–40, "This is the will of Him who sent Me, ... that everyone who looks to the Son and believes in Him shall have eternal life, and I will raise him up at the last day."

Postmillennialism ignores the scriptural teaching that Christians will face suffering and opposition to Christ until His Second Coming (Matt. 24:2–14, 37–51).

Seventh-Day Adventists

The Adventist movement of the 19th century emphasized the nearness of the Second Advent of Christ to establish His millennial kingdom. The main body to emerge from this movement was the Seventh-Day Adventists. They accept the Christian doctrines of the Trinity and the incarnation of the Son of God, unlike an Adventist group that emerged later, the Jehovah's Witnesses.

The Adventist expectations were initiated in 1831 by William Miller (1782–1849), who announced his discovery that Christ would return no later than March 21, 1844. When this date proved wrong, he revised it to October 22, 1844. His calculation was based on the prophecy of Dan. 8:14 that there were to be 2,300 days until the cleansing reconsecration of the sanctuary. He reckoned that the 2,300 days symbolized years in the Jewish calendar (either from March to March, or from October to October) and must be counted from 457 B.C.

October 22, 1844, became the "Great Disappointment" for Miller's followers. But some of them took the position that his calculation was correct but his interpretation was not. The "sanctuary" was not the earth but a sanctuary in heaven. Christ entered into this at the appointed date to begin the Last Judgment, a long investigation that is still in process. These people formed the Seventh-Day Adventist Church. (This and all other date-setting speculations about events of the Last Day runs counter to Jesus' words in Matt. 24:36.)

Source of Doctrine

The Adventists claim that while their teachings have a foundation in Scripture, their interpretations are divinely confirmed by the alleged revelations of Ellen White, their "prophetess." The meaning of the event of 1844 was given in one of her 2,000 or so visions.

Judgment and Salvation

According to traditional Adventist teaching, the Investigative Judgment was symbolized in the Old Testament by the cleansing of the sanctuary on the Day of Atonement (Lev. 16). Just as once a year the high priest entered the Holy of Holies to cleanse the people by removing their sins with blood and transferring those sins to the scapegoat sent into the wilderness, so Jesus began in 1844 to finish the work of atonement from sin begun on the cross.

Going over the record of each person's life, He gives a favorable verdict to all who have believed and committed themselves to God in love. He applies His blood to them and transfers their sin to Satan, who is the scapegoat that bears them. This means that the good works of the Christians qualify them for eternal life. Accordingly, Adventists put much stress on rules and regulations, including the Old Testament tithe and dietary rules and a strict health program that often includes vegetarianism.

Sabbatarianism

The name Seventh-Day Adventists indicates a belief that God requires observance of the seventh-day Sabbath (Saturday). Most of Christendom, they say, has sinfully abandoned the day of worship appointed by the divine law, and this could result in receiving an unfavorable verdict in the Investigative Judgment. (But they and other Sabbatarian bodies do not understand that the Sabbath law was given only to the Jews, Ex. 16:25; 20:9–10; 31:12–13; Ezek. 20:12. Christ freed us from the Jewish ceremonial laws, Heb. 8:6–7, especially the Sabbath days, Col. 2:16. This commandment contains both moral law and ceremonial law.)

The Afterlife

Adventists teach that life after death is conditional on one's worthiness. All who die enter into an unconscious soul sleep in the grave. Christ will determine in the Investigative Judgment whether one deserves to be immortal. Some, then, will be raised at the beginning of the millennium to reign with Christ. But the wicked will be raised at the end of the millennium only to be annihilated. There is no eternal experience of God's wrath in hell. (But see Phil 1:23; Matt. 8:12; 25:46.)

Dispensationalism

This popular kind of millennialism is found in the Pentecostal bodies, the Perfectionist bodies, many Baptist churches, and other groups. It is the view that the history of the world is divided into seven dispensations, conveniently corresponding to the divisions of the week.

The Seven Dispensations

The dispensationalist form of millennialism began in the 19th century with John Nelson Darby of the Plymouth Brethren. It has spread to many parts of Protestantism. The best-known source book is the Schofield Reference Bible, which defines a dispensation as "a period of time during which man is tested in respect to his obedience to some specific revelation of the will of God."

Dispensationalists usually speak of seven dispensations (seven periods of time). They are the periods of Innocence, Conscience, Human Government, Promise, the Law, the Church, and the Millennial Kingdom. In each period, they say, God has a new revelation and a different way of dealing with humanity to help and save them. They say that we are living the sixth dispensation (the Church) and that God now deals with us on the basis of the Gospel of grace. But they believe that in the next dispensation God will deal with us on the basis of the Gospel of the kingdom, which will have the Sermon on the Mount as its core.

Exaltation of Israel

Adventists understand Old Testament prophecies to mean that the Jews will accept the Messiah and will reign with Him over the whole world in a kingdom headquartered in Jerusalem. The establishment of the present state of Israel is the beginning of the fulfillment of these prophecies, and we can expect that it will eventually recognize Jesus as the Messiah. In the millennium God will relate Himself to Israel on the basis of a new national covenant, and the Old Testament ceremonial law will be reinstated in a rebuilt temple (Ezek. 40:48). Israel has not yet carried out the purpose assigned to it in Is. 49:6 of being a light to the Gentiles and will be enabled to do this in the Great Tribulation and the millennium.

The Kingdom Postponed

Dispensationalism is a form of millennialism that interprets the details of Revelation 20 literally, especially verse 6, "They will be priests of God and of Christ and will reign with him for a thousand years." They take this as a visible kingdom of earthly glory, splendor, and peace. They understand many prophecies from the rest of the Bible to be giving literal descriptions of the social, political, economic, religious, and geophysical conditions of that time. They interpret the two resurrections of Revelation 20 as referring to a resurrection of Christians and then, after a thousand years, a resurrection of unbelievers.

Dispensationalists teach that the events of the end times will be as follows:

A Secret Second coming of Christ for the Rapture, in which all Christians, still living or risen from the dead, will disappear from the world and be taken to heaven

The Great Tribulation, when the Antichrist will arise as a world dictator and persecute Jews and Gentiles who come to faith

The third coming of Christ to judge the Gentiles and establish His millennial reign

The thousand years, during which many messianic prophecies will be literally fulfilled and the Old Testament ceremonial laws will be reestablished

A final coming of Christ at the end of the millennium to raise the unbelievers, carry out the Last Judgment, and make a new heaven and a new earth

The Dispensationalists make a sharp distinction between the kingdom of God and the kingdom of Christ. The kingdom of God is the Christian church, while the kingdom of Christ is the visible and earthly kingdom of the Messiah in Jerusalem. The kingdom of Christ and the messianic age do not yet exist. Jesus expected to establish the throne of David at His first coming, but because of the insurmountable opposition of the Jews, He postponed the messianic kingdom to the time of the millennium and set up a different kingdom, the kingdom of God, or the church. This started a new dispensation, the dispensation of the church, which will end when the church is raptured.

Scripture rejects the idea that there are different dispensations and that during each God saves people in a different way. God has provided only one way of salvation throughout the Old and New Testaments. Peter describes this in Acts 10:43: "All the prophets testify about Him that everyone who believes in Him receives forgiveness of sins through His name." Thus, the Old Testament contains promises pointing forward to the Messiah; Old Testament people based their faith on these promises. And Romans 4 makes no distinction between Abraham's faith and our faith.

Scripture also rejects the teaching of a special destiny and exaltation of the Jews in the kingdom of Christ. In Gal. 3:28 God says, "There is neither Jew nor Greek, slave nor free, male nor female, for you are all one in Christ Jesus." Furthermore, according to Eph. 2:12–15, Christ has broken down the wall of partition between Jew and Gentile. Also, the ceremonial law of the Old Covenant will not be reinstituted. This would be contrary to Heb. 7:18: "The former regulation is set aside," and Heb. 8:13, where the author, after quoting Jer. 31:31–34, says, "By calling this covenant 'new,' He has made the first one obsolete; and what is obsolete and aging will soon disappear." It is not right to say that the kingdom of Christ and the Messianic age do not yet exist, because Jesus the Messiah has come and God has raised Him up to sit on His throne, as Peter says in the Pentecost sermon (Act 2:30).

Something to Think About

1. Describe religious liberalism. Why is it deplorable?

2. What is unionism? What problems do we face if we practice it?

3. Describe the cooperative alliances mentioned in this chapter and evaluate them in the light of Scripture.

4. Name some union churches and explain the problem with their approach.

5. What is the Restorationist movement? What is wrong with it?

6. What guidelines do you follow as you attempt to follow God's will in Christian liberty?

7. Explain premillennialism and postmillennialism. What are some problems with those teachings?

8. As its name indicates, Seventh-Day Adventism stresses the Second Advent of Christ. What ideas about the Last Things and the way of salvation does it add to premillennialism? In what ways does Scripture disagree?

9. How would you answer a Seventh-Day Adventist who says to you, "Your church has departed from scriptural teaching by not requiring worship on the seventh day of the week" (Ex. 20:8–10)?

10. Why is it comforting to know that Dispensationalism is wrong in its view about God's dealing with humanity?

8

Cults and Other Unchristian Groups

Historically, cults have been defined as groups that deny central articles of the Christian faith, such as the Trinity and the Incarnation. Groups fitting this definition include Jehovah's Witnesses and the Mormons.

During the last part of the 20th century—due in part to wide publicity connected to the Jonestown and Branch Dividian cults—some sociological uses of the term *cult* have followed a much narrower definition. As a result some Americans think of cults primarily as groups that use brainwashing techniques, live in isolation, and go to extremes in following a leader's instructions.

In this chapter we will follow the historic definition. Walter Martin states it as follows:

> A group of people gathered about a specific person or person's interpretation of the Bible.... From a theological viewpoint, the cults contain not a few major deviations from historic Christianity. Yet paradoxically, they continue to insist that they are entitled to be classified as Christians (*Kingdom of the Cults,* p. 11).

Most cults

deviate significantly from Christian teachings;

follow a specific person or person's interpretation of the Bible;

claim that they are entitled to be called Christians.

In this chapter we will also briefly examine the New Age Movement and forerunners of that movement. In those groups we find Christian ideas mixed with ideas that come from Hinduism, Buddhism, and other Eastern religions.

Unitarian-Universalists

The Unitarian and Universalist bodies in America have been merged since 1961 into the Unitarian-Universalist Association. Each originally became part of a trend in church history that appeared first in Europe and then in America.

The first trend—Unitarianism—is a denial of the Holy Trinity. American Unitarianism had roots in Europe. For example, Faustus Socinus spread unitarian ideas in Poland in the 16th century. The American form developed primarily among the Congregationalists, who tolerated doctrinal deviations and nonconfessional churchmanship. Preachers like William Ellery Channing (1780–1842) argued that God is not more than one person, that Christ is not the incarnation of God, and that we do not need a vicarious atonement for sin. These groups formed the American Unitarian Association in 1825.

The other trend—Universalism—is the denial of endless punishment. Its proponents rejected passages like 2 Thess. 1:9 and Matt. 25:46. They insisted that the restoration of all things promised in Acts 3:21 must include a restoration of every human being to harmony with God. They teach universal salvation.

The American Universalist body had its beginning in 1785. Some of their leaders, like John Murray (1741–1815), also accepted the Trinity and redemption through the blood and merit of Christ. Others, like Hosea Ballou (1771–1852; often called the father of American Universalism), denied these points. Over the years the Universalists became more and more like the Unitarians, following Ballou's lead.

Religious Liberalism

Unitarians and Universalists have often identified themselves as liberals, proudly emphasizing their claim of freedom from creed, tradition, and authority. This liberalism has grown wider and wider over the years. The "position statements" of the Unitarian-Universalist Association advocate a form of religious humanism. It views religion as an ever-evolving expression of human reason and experience.

The Unitarian Angle

Unitarian-Universalists and many other cults have usually reduced the Trinity into a unipersonal being, like breaking two angles off a triangle. By doing so they have broken themselves off from biblical Christianity.

Scripture teaches that there is but one God (1 Cor. 8:4), and yet there are three distinct persons, Father, Son, and Holy Spirit, each of whom is God (John 15:26; 1 Cor. 8:6; John 1:1; Acts 5:3–4). They are one in divine essence and should be honored equally (John 10:30; 5:27).

The heart of the Christian faith is that we have a divine Savior (Is. 43:11; John 1:14; Acts 20:28). This is an offense and stumbling block to reason, so some turn to unitarianism. They denounce the Three in One as bad mathematics and unenlightened religion. But the truly wise are not surprised to find that the true God and unlimited Savior cannot be measured by human reason, since He is not a creature of their own thought.

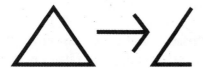

We see their use of reason in their arguments that a triune God and endless punishment are irrational and incompatible with their conceptions of the nature of God and the dignity of man. This rationalistic principle has been applied to every doctrine of the Christian religion.

Unitarian-Universalists often quote the Bible to make points about their religion, but they feel completely free to decide whether or not to recognize any idea as a biblical truth. They hold certain basic beliefs in common, such as freedom from fixed truth, the supreme worth of every human personality, the perfectibility of human beings, salvation by character, and the obligation to work for a world community of brotherhood and peace. One common Unitarian slogan in the past was "The Fatherhood of God, the brotherhood of man, the leadership of Christ, the progress of mankind upward and onward forever."

A Unitarian statement a few years ago said it this way:

> Do Unitarians believe in anything? We believe in brotherhood, in civil rights, in the U.N., in upgrading our educational system, in an attack upon the problems of poverty, in the nuclear test ban treaty.... Many of us even believe in God. (*The Hamburg Sun.* June 10, 1965)

God

Unitarian-Universalists agree that God is not triune and that Jesus is not God. Beyond this, they hold a variety of ideas. For instance, they may believe that Jesus is an exalted man, or that he was once an angelic being, or that God is a person, or that everything is God, or that we cannot know for sure if there is a God, or that *God* is a word for an abstract ideal.

Salvation by Character

Unitarian-Universalists believe that humanity is basically good. We don't need a Savior to die for our sins. But we do need to work at correcting our errors and solving our problems. We can achieve at least an earthly happiness, and, if a life after death is recognized, heavenly rewards.

Universalism

Some have said that Unitarianism and Universalism fit well together. The Unitarians teach that humanity is too good to be eternally damned, and the Universalists say that God is too good to damn people eternally. Today many of them would say that there is no God to damn anybody.

People in this groups hold various views, but they all agree that there is no everlasting punishment after death. Some say that there is only temporary punishment for sinners; others say that everyone goes immediately to heaven at death; and still others say that there is no life after death.

Premillennial Cults

Some cults have combined their errors with premillennial expectations.

Jehovah's Witnesses

Charles Taze Russell (1852–1916) started a Bible class in 1870 that grew into the group now known as the Jehovah's Witnesses. It has continued his teachings, though they have been modified over the years. The Watchtower Society, founded by Russell for publishing *The Watchtower* magazine and the other literature of the Witnesses, governs the body with a tight control.

Source of Doctrine

The Witnesses claim that the Bible is the source of their teaching and that their leaders have received special divine guidance to interpret it. Russell said that the Scriptures would remain dark apart from his writings. His successor, Joseph Rutherford (1869–1942), claimed to be the voice of God for his age. Witnesses believe that the Watchtower Society speaks as a prophet. The many changes of interpretation that have come about show that the prophetic guidance has not always been operating.

The Witnesses have produced their own version of the Bible, the New World Translation. It translates passages in a way that supports their teaching that Jesus and the Holy Spitit are not God in the same sense that the Father is God.

God

The Witnesses denounce the doctrine of the Trinity as a pagan concept of a "three-headed god." They teach that there is one divine person, Jehovah. The group derives its name from the New World Translation of Is. 43:10 ("You shall be My witnesses, says Jehovah") and from their claim to testify to the truth about Him.

The Witnesses argue that the Son of God is a creature, namely, Michael the archangel, and that the Holy Spirit is merely a name for the power of God. The Son was transformed from an angelic being into a human being at His

The Watchtower

This emblem of the Jehovah's Witnesses appears on their official magazine, The Watchtower, which has been published since 1879. It expresses the claim of the leaders of the Witnesses to be watchmen on a tower, as the prophets of the Old Testament were called (Jer. 6:17; Ezek. 3:17).

Watchmen are to look for and to announce dangers and godsends, warning and preparing the people. But the teachings of the Watchtower remind us of Is. 56:10, "Israel's watchmen are blind, they all lack knowledge." They have not seen the truths of God's Word and have not called people to true repentance and faith.

In fact, the church desperately needs true watchmen to warn against works-righteousness, denials of Christ's deity and bodily resurrection, and the other false doctrines of Jehovah's Witnesses and the cults.

conception and then back into a spiritual being at His death. He, they contend, is never called "God" in Scripture in the sense of the title that belongs to Jehovah, but only in the sense of a mighty creature. (A comparison of Rev. 22:12–16, 20 with 1:8 shows that this teaching is completely false.)

Christ's Resurrection and Return

The Witnesses teach that since Christ was changed back into an invisible spiritual being, He had only a "spiritual resurrection" and His body remains in the grave. His second advent began in 1914, with His action to set up the headquarters of His kingdom in heaven. This date was determined by applying an allegorical interpretation and calculation to Dan. 4:23. Witnesses say that His kingdom did not exist before this time. (But see Col. 1:13 and Acts 2:30–36.)

The heavenly part of the kingdom of Christ, they teach, is made up of 144,000 persons (described in Rev. 7:1–8), who are resurrected as spirit beings like Christ and rule with Him. The mission of Jehovah's Witnesses, both those of the 144,000 still alive and their co-workers, is to proclaim that Jehovah has now established the kingdom of Christ. Soon, after the battle of Armageddon, He will put it into operation as a millennial government on earth.

Jehovah's Witnesses have long been known for their ceaseless house calls to win people to their views and expectations. They have tried numerous times, unsuccessfully, to predict the date of Armageddon.

Salvation by Works

The Witnesses teach that through Adam all his descendants lost the right to live on earth and were doomed to die and pass out of existence. (There is no everlasting experience of God's wrath.) By His perfect obedience Christ earned for Himself the right to live. But He gave it up, ceasing to be a human being, in order to purchase for humanity the opportunity to obtain it. Jehovah will therefore bestow Christ's right to live on all who show themselves worthy of it by their lives and works.

During the millennium, most people will have the opportunity to pass the test of obedience and receive this justification. But already in this life the 144,000 earn their right to live on earth. They forfeit this right to become rulers in heaven. Some people are too wicked to be raised at all in the millennium. All others will live in the millennial kingdom and be given a chance to show their worthiness. All who fail will be annihilated. (Of course, these teachings about the millennium are contrary to Scripture. See the discussion of millennialism in chapter 7.)

The Worldwide Church of God

This cult, often known as the Worldwiders, is similar to the Jehovah's Witnesses. It was founded in 1934 by the radio preacher Herbert W. Armstrong. It has spread through the radio and television program *The World Tomorrow* and the magazine *The Plain Truth*.

Like the Witnesses, the Worldwide Church of God (WCG) denies the Trinity and the physical resurrection of Jesus, and teaches a salvation by works, a probation in the millennium, and annihilationism. They also teach that God is a family of gods or spirit beings. One of these is the eternal Son of God, who turned into a man for a short time. The goal of justification is to earn transformation into a spirit being and thereby become a member of the God Family.

The WCG also adheres to Anglo-Israelism (or British Israelism). They observe Jewish holidays and teach that the Anglo-Saxons are literal descendants of the 10 lost tribes of Israel. A racist tendency in these groups views Anglo-Saxons as the "master race." Some members are associated with the Ku Klux Klan and Neo-Nazism. (But see Jer. 50:1–4. The "lost tribes" are not lost.)

Mormons (Latter-Day Saints)

This body, known officially as the Church of Jesus Christ of Latter-Day Saints, was founded in 1830 by Joseph Smith (1807–77). He held that all existing churches had lost the true

Gospel, and he claimed to be restoring the church founded by Christ.

Smith established headquarters for his church successively at Kirtland, Ohio, Independence, Mo., and Nauvoo, Ill. He and his followers generated continuing controversy. Finally he and his brother and co-worker Hyrum were

Joseph Smith

jailed and then shot by a mob. The majority of the Mormons chose Brigham Young as Smith's successor and followed him to Salt Lake City, Utah. This city eventually became the center of a great religious and social empire.

Some rebel factions, however, refused Young's leadership and became separate Mormon bodies. The largest of these is the Reorganized Church of Jesus Christ of Latter-Day Saints. The chief doctrines of the Salt Lake City group are described below.

Source of Doctrine

The Mormons claim to follow the true interpretation of the Bible. In addition, Smith and other leaders after him called themselves prophets, receiving numerous revelations to authorize new doctrines and practices. The most famous is *The Book of Mormon*, from

---

Moroni

This portrayal of Moroni often appears on the covers of The Book of Mormon.

According to the "prophet" Joseph Smith, Moroni was an "angel" (a glorified person from the past). Smith declared that Moroni appeared to him in 1823 and informed him of the existence of 24 golden plates buried in the earth near his home at Palmyra, N.Y. These contained the hieroglyphic writing of the angel's father, Mormon. Smith translated this by means of mysterious stones and published it as The Book of Mormon.

The book claims to tell the history and religion of a civilization in America up to the year A.D. 428. It teaches salvation by works and other doctrines. It also contains prophesies about the United States, the coming of Joseph Smith, and the millennial kingdom of the last days.

The Book of Mormon does not teach polytheism or plural marriage. The Reorganized Church and other Mormon splinter groups accept The Book of Mormon but not the "revelations" of the Salt Lake City body that contain these doctrines.

which their nickname comes. Other teachings are published in *The Pearl of Great Price* and *Doctrines and Covenants*. (See the solemn warning in Jer. 23:31.)

God

Mormons believe that there are many gods, none of whom is a divine being. The most important, who is usually meant when the name *God* is used, is the Father. He is an exalted man, who was born at some time in the distant past and later glorified. Therefore they say, "As man is, God once was; as God is, man may become." God has a body and begets children by his wife. The two most prominent of these, who have become gods along with him, are the Son and the Holy Ghost. (It is plain that none of these is the God of the Bible, with neither beginning nor end—Ps. 90:2; Hos. 11:9.)

Salvation

Mormons teach that all human beings have a preexistent life in the Father's home as spirit beings born in his family. They then come to be born on earth with physical bodies, in order to have the opportunity to earn godhood. Sin has separated them from God. But the Son of God (an exalted and deified creature referred to in the previous section) was born into a human body and made atonement for them, so that they could be restored to God's presence and have the possibility of gaining salvation according to the law and justice.

The Articles of Faith in *The Pearl of Great Price* state: "We believe that through the atonement of Jesus Christ all mankind may be saved by obedience to the laws and ordinances of the Gospel" (p. 67). The doctrine of justification by faith alone is denounced as sectarian and evil. (Contrast this with Rom. 3:23–28!)

Mormons teach that some will succeed in becoming gods by their works and will rule on earth during the millennium and on their own personal planets thereafter. Others will achieve lesser degrees of glory. All who are not in the kingdom of heaven will have to pay for their sins in hell-fire, but this suffering will eventually come to an end. (But see Matt. 25:46.)

The future gods expect to raise families in the millennium and afterwards. For this reason they seal women to themselves in "celestial marriages" in the Mormon temples. The more wives, the better. In fact, this is considered a requisite for attaining godhood. (But see Matt. 22:30.)

The Church

Joseph Smith alleged that he was called to reestablish the church of Christ, which had disappeared on the earth. It must have both an Aaronic priesthood and a Melchizedek priesthood. (But see Matt. 16:18.) Mormons teach that only the true church can administer valid sacraments. So they perform thousands of proxy baptisms for the dead who have no true baptism and are in hell. These can then enter the kingdom of heaven. (But see Luke 16:26; Heb. 9:27.)

The Science Religions

The science religions are cults that claim the Bible contains a system of science that can enable a person to achieve health, success, and happiness. Their doctrine is centered in the glorification of humanity. Some of the better-known groups will be briefly described here.

Christian Science

Mary Baker Eddy (1821–1910) organized the Church of Christ, Scientist in 1879. She appears to have been adopting and further developing the philosophy of Phineas Parkhurst Quimby, a healer who had treated her for her ailments. He claimed that he employed Christ's own system of healing by mental power. She asserted that she

Mary Baker Eddy

"Self-evident" Propositions?

In Science and Health *(p. 113) Eddy presented the following four propositions of her philosophy. She claimed that they could be seen to be "self-evident," because they could be stated backwards as well as forwards, like a mathematical equation.*

1. God is All-in-all.

2. God is good. Good is mind.

3. God, Spirit being all, nothing is matter.

4. Life, God, omnipotent Good deny death, evil, sins, disease.

These statements affirm that God is only a principle of reality. They deny that sin, matter, disease, and death really exist.

But Scripture gives a personality to the Lord of heaven and earth. We have a God who judges, a God who comforts, a God worthy of our faith, and a God who hears our prayers. See, for example, Is. 43:25; 2 Tim. 2:19; Ezek. 18:30; Heb. 1:3; Ps. 102:17.

Scripture clearly teaches the reality of the material world (Col. 1:16; Heb. 2:14), of sin (1 John 1:10), and of death (Ps. 104:29; Rom. 6:23). The Lord wants us to treat sickness as real (Matt. 25:36), even for the enlightened (Phil. 2:25–29; 1 Cor. 12:7–9).

The following "self-evident" propositions will serve us better.

1. The experience of "illusion" cannot be illusion.
   Philosophically, the Christian Science concept of illusions is self-destructive. If nothing could exist that is not God—and so matter and sin must be illusions—how could illusions exist, since God is not illusion? This "principle" will not help.

2. Sin, pain, sickness, and death are facts of life.

This is self-evident from human experience. The belief that we can use only faith in the Christ Idea—and never doctors and material aids—has often had tragic results in unnecessary suffering and death. Even Eddy and her followers have not consistently adhered to it. For instance, she sometimes allowed anesthetics, surgery, and the setting of broken bones.

Most people recognize the absurdity of the Christian Science idea. In the Georgia legislature a member once introduced an amendment to exempt Christian Scientists from the requirement to obtain a certificate showing they were free from venereal disease in order to get a marriage license. He said the requirement violated the Christian Science belief that venereal disease does not exist. In the debate that followed a legislator remarked that bacteria have no religion. See Ps. 121:2 for the true hope of deliverance.

had discovered the "science" that lay behind Christ's conquest of disease and all other evils. Christian Science practitioners (healers) continue to apply her theological claims and methods.

Source of Doctrine

According to Eddy, the Bible is filled with errors on the surface, but its underlying meaning is the truth of Christian Science. *Science and Health with Key to the Scriptures,* which she published in 1875, makes the allegorical content of Scripture clear. She claimed that it was of divine origin, though it went through a number of revisions. Readings from it are the "only preacher" in Christian Science services.

God

Eddy rejected the doctrine of the Trinity and taught instead that there is a triple divine principle: Life, Truth, and Love.

Though allegorically described as personal, deity should ultimately be regarded as the "all-in-all" and "all substance" (*Science and Health,* pp. 113, 587), the whole of reality, and also the "principle of scientific being" (p. 332). Man is a reflection of God and a part of God. Since God is the only being that exists at all, nothing can exist that is opposite to God's nature. Thus there is no matter, sin, sickness, or death (*Science and Health,* pp. 330–31).

Mary Baker Eddy said that she discovered these tremendous truths in 1866, at a time when she was suffering from injuries resulting from a fall on the ice. Reading Matt. 9:2–8, she was persuaded that Jesus healed the man sick of the palsy by convincing him the sickness did not exist. She claimed to heal herself by the same method.

Christ

In Christian Science, Christ is the Idea of Sonship, the truth that man is a "son" or part of God and therefore cannot have a body or be sick, mortal, or sinful. Jesus is the human soul that most fully grasped the Christ Idea and applied it for the benefit of Himself and others. His atonement is His work as the Way-shower in demonstrating how everyone can come to an effective realization that he or she is constantly "one with God"—in fact, is God.

Eddy taught that Jesus conquered the illusions that He encountered of material existence and death. Those who follow Him will be enabled by use of the Christ Idea to do the same for themselves and others. They will obtain remission of sin (as Christian Scientists conceive it), because they will destroy the illusion that their sin exists and will progressively display their perfect divine nature. (The contrast with the biblical teaching of the Incarnation and vicarious atonement is glaringly obvious.)

Prayer

According to Eddy and her followers, prayer can take the outward form of an address to a divine person. But in reality, they regard it as simply an affirmation of the Christ Idea and the truth about God, man, the world, disease, and death. This is how their practitioners pray for the sick.

New Thought

The Unity School of Christianity, the Church of Religious Science, the Divine Science Federation, and similar cults are examples of the New Thought Movement. Arising toward the end of the 19th century, they claim to be proclaiming a new and enlightened approach to religion and life.

Like Christian Science, they are influenced by the philosophy of P. P. Quimby, who asserted that sicknesses are effects of incorrect, negative thinking. They use much of the same terminology as Christian Science: God as impersonal principle, man as divine, prayer as affirmation, evils as unreal, etc.

But they embrace a different kind of pantheism. They hold that man is one in essence with God, but they do not deny that sin, trouble, sickness, and death actually exist. New Thought call these things "unreal" or "illusions." They mean that these conditions are not as important or unmanageable as they appear. They can be controlled by the power of the mind and the human being's divine energy.

Spiritualist Churches

Spiritists believe that a person with special psychic (soul) powers can communicate with the spirits of the dead. They also claim that the spirits can send messages to the living through such a medium or by such devices as rapping on tables or appearances in bodily form.

Spiritualists are spiritists who use Christian terminology or forms of worship, but with new meanings. For instance, the teaching of the Church of the New Jerusalem is based on what Emanuel Swedenberg claimed to learn in the spirit world—for instance, that the doctrines of the Trinity and justification through faith are false. The same often occurs in theosophical cults (see below).

There are several spiritualist churches, such as the National Spiritualist Association of Churches. They deny every basic doctrine of the Christian faith. According to them God is an impersonal force, the Infinite Intelligence, while Christ was a medium. After death a person's soul progresses to perfection.

Scripture warns against spiritism and all forms of witchcraft (Ex. 22:18; Lev. 19:31; Deut. 18:10–12). The dead are out of touch with the living (Is. 63:16; Eccl. 9:5–6). The psychic phenomena are often frauds, as is frequently proven by the Psychical Research Society. Or Spiritualists may perform tricks of demons, who have great power to make strange things happen (Matt. 4:5, 8; Acts 16:16–18). They welcome new opportunities to introduce "things taught by demons" (1 Tim. 4:1) in order to ruin souls.

New Age Religion

The Forerunners

The New Age Movement (NAM) consists of many groups that draw heavily upon concepts of Hinduism and Buddhism, as well as other metaphysical sources. These are often used to reinterpret Christian themes and ideas. The forerunners of this East-West mishmash were the theosophical groups. They are the Theosophical Society of America (founded 1875) and its various splinter groups and counterparts, such as the Church of Illumination and the Liberal Catholic Church. Some are simply American branches of Eastern religion, like the Vedanta Society. These groups still exist and can be regarded as one part of the NAM.

Theosophists adapt Eastern concepts such as Brahman (the pantheistic World Soul), reincarnation, and karma (causal connections governing the cycle of life and rebirth). These meanings are often poured into Christian terms. For instance, the atonement becomes realization that you are one with the World Soul.

New Age-ism

The modern New Age Movement is often said to have originated in 1971 with the publication of *Be Here Now,* by Baba Ram Dass, who began life as Richard Alpert. New Agers see themselves as harbingers of a new age for humanity. They seek transformation of individuals and of society as a whole. It has been heavily influenced by Hindu philosophy. The movement is loosely constituted, including many groups with differing teachings and beliefs but sharing certain themes, more or less. There are clusters of groups, loose networks of common ideas, conferences, workshops, journals, newsletters, coalitions, and political action groups. *The New Age Source Book* and *The New Age Directory* list thousands of groups. They include the following:

Self-development organizations (like Silva Mind Control and Forum)
Think tanks and communities (Findhorn, Esalen Institute, etc.)
Holistic health associations
Religious groups (New Age Church of Truth, Scientology, UFO cults, drug-using churches, etc.)
Hindu groups (Eckankar, Ananda Marga Yoga Society, etc.)

Ideas of New Age-ism

Not all people involved in the New Age Movement hold all these ideas, but all the ideas are important in New Age religion.

Pantheism

This says that all is God. God is not separate from the world. God is not a person, but an impersonal force or energy or consciousness that is in everything and identified with it somehow. Hinduism, with its concept of Brahman as the basic cosmic force, is commended for having found the truth.

The Christian response: God is separate from the universe, as its Creator and Judge. The creation has been corrupted, but not the Maker, who is perfectly holy. Only a perfectly good God can be relied upon to deal with wickedness and evil.

In the thinking of Pantheism, if all is God, then God is both good and bad. So, for example, the New Age leader Benjamin Creme says that the forces of good and the forces of evil are two aspects of God. Furthermore, if everything is God, anything is permissible. If the purpose of life is to express your divine nature, and God is both good and evil, you can justify anything you want to do. Moral relativism is often a feature of NAM.

Scripture teaches that God is a personal being. He judges, loves, keeps promises, etc. He has a personal name: the Lord, Yahweh. So Christians who are tempted to accept pantheism, New Age religion, or Hinduism, should be told that they are giving up the truths that God is perfectly good and that He is personal (that is, tripersonal).

Human Divinity

This flows out of Pantheism. God dwells within you as you. He is your Higher Self. Followers of this movement are often urged to repeat to themselves: "I am God." Enlightenment is realization of your oneness with God, the deity of your self. This is the basis of the self-help movements in NAM. The basic NAM attitude is this: "We are like gods and might as well get good at it."

Many admire Jesus as a man who realized his divinity and perfectly expressed it. He taught that all people can make the same self-discovery as He did and accomplish what He accomplished. The NAM calls upon every person to recognize that "the Messiah is within you," or to awaken to a "Christ consciousness" (which is nothing more than self-glorification).

The Christian response: "You will be like God" is Satan's old and great lie (Gen. 3:5). Humans cannot be God: we are sinful, limited, and need to repent and trust in God. See Ex. 28:2 and James 4:6. I am not my own Messiah or Savior—no mere human can be. Hindu and

New Age "enlightenment" is the discovery that you are God. The Gospel enlightenment is the knowledge that you are a sinner reconciled to God by the cross of Christ (2 Cor. 5:18–19; Rom. 5:10). The true transformation is described in 2 Cor. 5:17 and Ezek. 11:19. 2 Peter 1:3–4 shows how we really become like God.

Reincarnation

Many in the NAM have adopted the Hindu concept of reincarnation (that one is born again in one life after another). They claim to prove this by such things as deja vu experiences, memories of former lives by people under hypnosis, or the skill of some character actors (thought to be acting out the personalities of their former lives). Reincarnation, they say, gives unlimited opportunity to a soul to become enlightened and spiritually strong.

The Christian response: Reincarnation is a false hope (Heb. 9:27). It denies the existence of everlasting hell and the hope of resurrection of the body.

Cosmic Evolutionary Optimism

This belief states that humanity, being divine, is in charge of its own evolution and advancement. The next state of evolution will be the development of consciousness. The New Age will be the time of expanded consciousness and application of human potential. It is already beginning and will proceed to mass enlightenment and the establishment of social unity and peace. Astrology is widely used in NAM, and the New Age is often called the Age of Aquarius (the sign of the Water Bearer in the Zodiac). Many say that we are now in the time of transition between the Age of Pisces (sign of the Fish) and the Age of Aquarius.

The Christian response: New Age religion is false and corrupt, and therefore cannot produce a golden age. No new age of happiness is going to be brought about by New Age ideas. New Age religion really belongs to the old age of sin and unbelief.

Gal. 1:4: The "present evil age" is the period from the Fall to Judgment Day. Any "new age" fallen humanity brings about will remain part of the fallen, sinful age in which we now live.

Luke 16:8; 20:34: Some folks are people of this (evil) age, belong to it, and share in the evil characteristics of it.

1 Cor. 2:4: The devil is the power behind the moral spirit and darkness of this age.

1 Cor. 2:6–10: Some do not belong to this age, its corruption and curse.

Gal. 1:4: We Christians are freed from the corruption of this age.

Eph. 1:20–21: Christ rules in this age and the age to come.

Heb. 6:5: The Christians have already experienced the age to come—the real New Age.

Lev. 19:26; Is. 47:13: Astrology is false. One should seek guidance from God's Word and trust in Him instead of guiding one's life by baseless star-gazing ideas. Astrologers' forecasts, which are guesses, have frequently failed to come to pass.

Spirit Guidance

Many NAM leaders claim that messages have come from glorified beings or entities. Sometimes these entities have appeared to them. They say that these are gods that have come from the divine cosmic energy, or souls that don't have to reincarnate any more, or dead people who are contacted between reincarnations. The process of communicating by spirits through a human serving as a medium, or channel, is called channelling.

The Christian response: Consulting spirits is an abomination, forbidden to Christians (Deut. 18:10–12). The dead are in God's hands (Eccl. 12:7, 14). We have no power to summon or manipulate them. Alleged spirit contacts are either hoaxes or demonic appearances. Christians have the true Spirit guidance (John 16:13, 1 Cor. 2:13).

Holistic Health

Holistic health is the treatment of the whole person, not just the body, but also mind and spirit. Restoration of health depends on mental attitude. In New Age thinking holistic health is based on pantheism and the use of divine energy within human beings and creative forces at their disposal—"the healer inside us." Life force and energy flow need to be unblocked and directed.

Some claim to find the truth about healing in the non-Christian religions of China, India, and other cultures. We see a variety of ideas about techniques for achieving holistic, pantheist healing—acupuncture, acupressure, massage and bodywork therapy, guided imagery, psychic diagnosis, occult healing methods, yoga, hypnosis, and self-hypnosis.

Some Christians use the term *wholistic health* to describe their response. Spiritual and emotional factors, as well as physical factors, affect health. We should seek God's help in all sickness through faith and prayer. A Christian, cheerful mental and spiritual attitude can contribute to the prevention or cure of stress-related sickness (Ex. 15:26; Prov. 3:7–8; 15:30; 16:24; 17:22). But New Age pantheistic ideas of innate divine healing energies and life forces are unchristian. So are occultic notions of healing. Yoga is dangerous if the meditation involves Hindu or pantheistic ideas.

Hypnotism can involve unwholesome power over a subject, and its invasion of privacy may cause psychological and spiritual damage. Cases have been documented of people under hypnosis who were led to act contrary to their original moral beliefs.

Human Potential

Many followers of holistic health believe that the human being is god and therefore has great potential for revitalization, transformation, growth, improved memory, freedom, richness of life, and creativity. This is especially promoted in cultic programs or study centers like EST (now called Forum), the Esalen Institute in Big Sur, Calif., and certain schools of psychology.

Humanistic psychology is atheistic but says that humans are godlike. For example, Abraham Maslow (1908–70) said that there is a positive, self-activating force within each person, that one's inner nature is good or at least neutral, and that humans have unlimited potential.

Transpersonal psychology says that every person has a divine higher self. Such thinking is pantheistic. It is promoted in the California Institute of Transpersonal Psychology (Menlo Park, Calif.) and in a periodical, *The Journal of Transpersonal Psychology*.

The Christian response: One who trusts in the Lord's grace and help has great potential for an abundant, wonderful life (Ps. 37:4–6; Rom. 8:37; Phil. 4:13; Ps. 145:14; Titus 2:14). But we must reject self-deification. We are all corrupt, sinful beings.

Transformational Politics

Various political-action and lobby groups have been formed. They say that a new age, with a raised consciousness of humanity's godhood and potential, needs a politically transformed society. The agenda of many New Agers includes concerns about ecology, feminism, abortion rights, population control, and redistribution of wealth. The belief that all people have the same divinity leads to a call for political unity in which nationalism and patriotism are eliminated. They advocate international political sanctions, regulation of world culture, planetary taxation, and increased power for the United Nations.

Not all New Age political groups call for the same approach. Many call for decentralization of civil government (though still advocating the governmental measures that have been mentioned). Other groups, such as Planetary Citizens and World Goodwill (an organization connected with the Alice Bailey theosophical movement), call for a powerful one-world government.

The Christian response: Christians are indeed to be good citizens, do good to their neighbors, be peacemakers, and try to change what is wrong in the world (Gal. 6:9–10; Rom. 12:18; Prov. 14:31; 28:3). Some Christian citizens will agree with some New Age social goals but without the New Age presuppositions. But Christians cannot accept the New Age philosophy involved in New Age politics, or the justification of immoral practices by means of New Age thinking. They cannot share the cosmic optimism based on humanity's "divinity."

Testing the Doctrines

Christians have the responsibility to make the evaluation for which St. Paul calls in 1 Thess. 5:21: "Test everything. Hold on to the good." We will encounter many conflicting teachings of religious spokespersons and cannot avoid the need to make such a test. St. John writes, "Dear friends, do not believe every spirit, but test the spirits to see whether they are from God, because many false prophets have gone out into the world" (1 John 4:1). In this way one can decide personally which teaching and which church body deserves to be followed. We are also better prepared to teach children or others about such matters.

The Lutheran Confessions point out the instrument to be used in this testing. "Holy Scripture remains the only judge, rule, and norm according to which as the only touchstone all doctrines should and must be understood and judged as good or evil, right or wrong" (Tappert, p. 465). The Word of God will lead to finding the truth (John 8:31–32) and is the touchstone for testing the purity of the teachings in the church.

This course has been designed to help Christians carry out this test. We have provided explanations of church teachings and some touchstone Bible passages. This study of truth and error can help believers grow in Christ-centered knowledge (2 Peter 3:18) and more fully understand Christian doctrine (Heb. 6:1).

Moreover, the study of denominations will lead faithful Christians to a deeper appreciation of their own confessions and teachings. As they compare these with the Word of God, they will acquire a humble gratitude to God for the explanation and preservation of biblical truth among them. They will be able to declare wholeheartedly with signers of the Formula of Concord:

> This is the doctrine, faith, and confession of all of us as we shall give account of it on the Last Day before the righteous judge, our Lord Jesus Christ, and we shall neither secretly nor publicly say or write anything contrary to it but intend by the grace of God to abide by it. (Tappert, p. 500)

▼
Something to Think About

1. What do Unitarian-Universalists say about God and salvation? What would be lost if their contentions were true? How can you refute them?

2. Respond to the Universalist claim that Acts 3:21 states that all people will ultimately be saved.

3. Show that Jehovah's Witnesses are *not* witnessing to the truth about God.

4. What is wrong with attempts by Jehovah's Witnesses and others to calculate dates for events of the Last Times?

5. What do Mormons believe about God? Christ? hell? justification?

6. Why can the Latter-Day Saints doctrine about the church be troubling for someone who is not sure whether or not it is true?

7. What great biblical expectation is missing from the hope of the Worldwide Church of God?

8. Why are the Science religions so called? Compare 1 Tim. 6:20. What is the knowledge that we *really* need for blessing and happiness?

9. How does Christian Science deny biblical doctrines about God, Christ, sin, and death?

10. What does Christian Science teach about sickness? What does the Bible teach?

11. State in your own words the "self-evident" propositions of Christian Science. What is wrong with them?

12. Explain why a Christian should not believe that he or she is God.

13. Show that Spiritualism is unchristian.

14. Contrast the theosophic ideas about God and atonement with what you believe.

15. Mention ideas found in the New Age Movement. For each idea explain in your own words how to respond to it as a Christian.

16. What do you think attracts people to the Jehovah's Witnesses? the Mormons? Christian Science? New Age religion?

17. What are three significant insights you have gained during this course?

Helps for the Leader

This course contains materials for discussing the church bodies of America. You may have a strong background in this area. Or you may not have thought much about the teachings of these groups. Perhaps some of them will be new to you, and some may seem very strange.

Whatever the case, you and the group can gain much through this study. You will be considering what some are saying about your God and His will, sometimes disagreeing with one another. And you have the assurance that you have a reliable and indispensable instrument for understanding and evaluating all these ideas. This is the guide of which Ps. 119:105 speaks: "Your Word is a lamp to my feet and a light for my path."

May God use His Word to give you ever more of the light of the knowledge of His truth and grace in Christ, and may He make you able to speak His Word to all who can be helped by hearing it!

Some Guidelines for Conducting the Class

Begin each session with prayer, adding a hymn or psalm or other element of worship if desired. Always ask the Lord to give you a heart of love for the people whose beliefs you will be studying and wisdom to relate to them. You may wish to choose hymns or Bible readings that refer to one or more doctrines that will be discussed in the session. Brief comments about these teachings may be a useful introduction to later discussions.

Ask the participants to follow the guidelines in the Introduction as they prepare for a session. They should read the chapter, think through the questions printed there—jotting down some answers if they wish—and bring with them other questions about the churches or doctrines mentioned in the chapter.

Work through the questions with the participants. Add to or clarify their answers as needed. Perhaps follow an individual's answer with another question, e.g., "Would anyone else like to comment on that?" or "Does everyone agree with that?" Allow time to discuss questions that participants bring. Also prepare questions you wish to discuss.

You may wish to expand on some of the material presented in a chapter. Also plan to study some of the Bible passages cited and related passages that you may wish to suggest. At times you may wish to apply the exercise described in "Adding and Subtracting" (in chapter 1) to the doctrine of the group you are studying. This exercise involves marking pluses or minuses in the text.

Encourage the participants to comment about the material. Draw out their thoughts about what they have read and learned. They may have personal experiences to relate about relatives or acquaintances in other churches, or about their own previous background in another denomination.

Help members of your group examine the implications of the false teachings of the various groups. Not only do those false doctrines disagree with the certain Word of truth revealed in Scripture. They also rob members of blessings God gives us through the Gospel. For each church body you might ask, "How do the teachings of this group threaten a blessing God gives to us?"

You may not always be prepared or able to give answers to the questions that participants raise. Do not worry about this, since they will not expect you to be omniscient. Deal with the questions as well as you can. If possible, relate them to the themes of the Christian faith. At times you probably will want to consult other resources for answers and report your findings at a future time. The group will appreciate your efforts.

Give some attention to the implications of the course for the work of church school teachers. Ask what parts of the material studied would be helpful for children of various ages. Explore ways to illustrate and explain what different groups teach, and develop suggestions for making contrasts between true and false doctrine.

Before the participants leave, remind them to look over the material for the next session. Encourage them to have a concerned (and, as much as possible, a sympathetic) interest in the faith of their neighbors.

Helps for Answering the Questions

Chapter 1

Note that we have not provided suggested responses for questions that call for personal reaction or opinion.

Question 1. Separations have come about because of disagreements over teachings, such as the Trinity, the deity of Christ, and justification. Other factors, including historical circumstances and personality clashes, have also played a part in the formation and continued existence of separate groups. The "Family Tree" chart show some of the developments.

Question 2. See the section "Why We Should Deplore Divisions." Also remember that those who defend the truth of God's Word must refuse to unite with those who attack it (Rom. 16:17; 2 John 10–11).

Question 3. See the section "The Teaching Task of the Church of Christ." In carrying out this task we honor God both as Judge and Redeemer. We show the human race how to find peace, guidance, and wholeness of life.

Question 4. Committed Christians will want to remain faithful to God and will also want others to do so. Therefore we will insist that our church follow God's will, conscientiously spread His saving message, know Him as He wants to be known, and express trust in Christ alone for salvation.

Question 6. The "holy Christian church" in the creeds is made up of all who believe in Jesus Christ as Savior. The denominational "churches" are visible groups formed for the purpose of confession of faith and service to God. They are communities within which the one church of believers can be found.

Question 7. Yes, "God's way" does exist. He has revealed it to us in His Word (2 Tim. 3:16).

Question 9. The Apostles' Creed summarizes the teaching of the apostles. The Nicene Creed states the teaching of the Council of Nicea (A.D. 325). The Athanasian Creed is named in honor of St. Athanasius, a spokesperson for the deity of Christ. *Ecumenical,* or worldwide, means "expressing the faith held by the Christian church throughout the world."

Question 10. Statements that follow are from the Apostles' Creed (Ap), Nicene Creed (N), and the Athanasian Creed (Ath).

Against Judaizers and all teachers of salvation by works: "Crucified also for us" (N); "suffered for our salvation" (Ath).

Against the Gnostics: "One God" (N); "Maker of heaven and earth" (Ap, N); "born . . . suffered . . . died . . . rose" (Ap, N, Ath); "human flesh" (Ath).

Against Arius: "God of very God . . . of one substance with the Father" (N); "God and man; God of the substance of the Father" (Ath).

Against Macedonius: "Lord and giver of life . . . worshiped and glorified" (N); "the Holy Spirit is God" (Ath).

Against Pelagius: "Giver of life" (N)—that is, the Spirit must give us spiritual life.

Against Nestorius; "Although His is God and man, yet His is not two by one Christ" (Ath).

Against Eutyches: "God and man . . . perfect God and perfect man" (Ath).

Question 11. Originating in the Old World: Eastern Orthodox, Roman Catholic, Lutheran, Presbyterian, Episcopalian, Baptist, Mennonite, Methodist, and others. Originating in the New World: Disciples of Christ, Christian Science, Seventh-Day Adventists, Jehovah's Witnesses, Mormons, and others.

Question 12. The pope was said to have God-given authority to endorse this false doctrine of salvation, and submission to the pope was a work done for the sake of salvation.

Question 13. The saving faith in the heart may be inconsistent with the false doctrine in the person's head (the "happy inconsistency").

Question 14. See "The Christian at the Whirlpool."

Question 15. Church bodies are grouped as Lutheran, ancient traditions (Eastern Orthodox; Roman Catholic), Calvinist reformation, Arminian, churches rejecting infant baptism, union churches, and cults and other unchristian groups.

Chapter 2

Question 1. *Evangelical* emphasizes belief in the Gospel (*evangel*) of salvation by grace through faith and not by works.

Question 2. *Symbol* means mark of identification. It is important to have Lutheran Symbols, which can be used to determine whether teachers claiming to be Lutheran actually are.

Question 3. The Lutheran Confessions do not claim to add any teaching that Scripture lacks. Scripture contains all that is necessary for the life of the Christian and the work of the church. It is God's Word and thoroughly equips us (2 Tim. 3:16–17).

Question 4. The Lutheran confessions conform to Scripture at every point of teaching.

Question 5. To pledge subscription to the Lutheran Confessions "insofar as" they agree with Scripture allows one to teach one or more doctrines that disagree with the Confessions and Scripture.

Question 6. "The Word of God shall establish articles of faith, and no one else, not even an angel" (Tappert, p. 295). That is, we should not expect that God will ever send a man or an angel to tell us that His Word is wrong on some point.

Question 8. The Reformation continued the emphasis of the 95 Theses on repentance and the sinner's total dependence on Christ and God's grace.

Question 9. The Law cannot save; it shows our sin and our need for a Savior. The Gospel declares God's action through Christ for our salvation. The Law demands righteousness—which we do not have. The Gospel bestows Christ's righteousness to be counted as ours. The Law cannot make us Christian. The Gospel creates saving faith. The Law cannot bring about true obedience to its divine commands. The Gospel kindles love for God and a desire to please Him.

Question 10. Both statements have been defended and rejected by various people. Scripture teaches that good works are not necessary for salvation. But good works *are* necessary because of God's will and command.

Question 11. The Gospel brings liberation and spiritual health. Christian liberty is freedom from slavery to sin and from the compulsion and condemnation of the Law. It is freedom from the false opinions that salvation is gained by works and that the basis of a right relationship with God includes obedience to laws He has not commanded. Faith can insist on liberty to do as one pleases in things God has neither commanded nor forbidden, and love is willing to refrain temporarily from this liberty to avoid confusing one whose faith is weak (1 Cor. 8:9–11).

Question 12. The means of grace are the means by which God offers and bestows forgiveness and the benefits of redemption. They are the Word of God (including the pronouncement of absolution), Baptism, and the Lord's Supper.

Question 13. In Christ's church a child of God has fellowship with Him, continuous forgiveness, and the rights and privileges of a royal priesthood.

Question 14. There is boundless comfort in knowing that one's salvation is in God's hands from all eternity, that it is not caused by any good in ourselves but rests on God's grace in Christ.

Question 15. See the section "The Church."

Chapter 3

Question 1. When church teachers argue that some doctrine is oral tradition not preserved in the Scriptures, they are in fact asking us to base faith and practice on their claim that this is so. But the Lord expects His church to use the Scriptures as the final norm (2 Tim. 3:15–16; Acts 17:10–11). He has not changed the doctrine of Scripture, or added to it, in oral tradition. Therefore we have a sure safeguard against all such notions as purgatory, salvation by works, prayer to saints, the sinlessness of the Virgin Mary, or the divine right of the pope to be head of the church.

Question 2. See sections about "The Church" under Eastern Orthodoxy and Roman Catholicism. If we say that membership in Christ's church depends upon a denominational organization, we are distorting teachings about salvation and denying Christian liberty in matters not commanded by God, such as church government and organization.

Question 3. The papacy is the office of the head of the church. See "The Papal Seal" in chapter 3 and "The church in Ancient Times" in chapter 1. Scripture supports none of the claims.

Question 4. See "The Way of Salvation" under Eastern Orthodoxy. Scripture teaches that fallen sinners have no freedom of the will in spiritual matters and that we are justified through faith alone.

Question 5. This teaching disagrees with God's Word. It dishonors the Savior and His work. We would never have honest assurance that our own works and sufferings are sufficient payment. We would lose the comfort of the Gospel.

Question 6. Lutherans teach that saving grace is the unmerited favor of God. Roman Catholics teach that it is God-given help to pay for sin and merit eternal life.

Question 7. Both view the sacraments as supplying grace for justification through faith and works. They are Baptism, Confirmation, Eucharist, Penance, Ordination, Matrimony, and Anointing of the Sick. Lutherans hold that only three are means of grace: Baptism (Matt. 28:19); Eucharist (Matt. 26:26–28); and Penance, or Confession and Absolution (John 20:22–23).

Question 8. It is contrary to Scripture and turns us away from complete reliance on Christ.

Question 9. While both believe in the real presence of Jesus' body and blood, serious difference exist: Rome teaches—contrary to Scripture—the doctrine of transubstantiation (bread and wine are changed into body and blood; bread and wine are no longer present), holds that wine can properly be withheld from lay people, and teaches that the body and blood of Jesus in the Eucharist can be used for a sacrifice for sin.

Question 10. Pluralism allows diversity of teaching. See the section on pluralism.

Question 11. It is the concept that people can be saved without using and believing the name of Jesus or professing the faith of Christianity.

Chapter 4

Question 1. See the section on "Statements of the Calvinist Heritage."

Question 2. Calvinist tradition teaches predestination of some to damnation and also limited atonement and availability of grace. Lutheran theology teaches universal grace. Note the different—and false—picture of God painted by the Calvinist view.

Question 3. The Bible teaches that Christ died for all.

Question 4. Immediate grace is forgiveness and life that are bestowed without the means of Word and Sacrament. Almost all non-Lutheran Protestant bodies accept this view. See the section "The Means of Grace."

Question 5. Calvinists oppose the Lutheran doctrine that the Lord's Supper is a means by which God conveys the benefits of grace. Also, they do not agree with Lutherans that the body and blood of the Lord are really present in the Supper, strengthen faith, and bring the forgiveness He has earned for them. This is related to the idea that Christ's humanity cannot be in heaven and on earth at the same time.

Question 6. The Episcopalian system is government of the church by bishops. The Presbyterian is government by presbyters (elders). The Congregationalist (held by Congregationalists, Baptists, Disciples of Christ, and others) is self-government by congregations. We need to know that Scripture does not prescribe any specific type of government. Thus, some Lutherans use bishops, and others use a form of congregationalism.

Question 7. The Law does not bring grace or forgiveness or assurance or sanctification. A person who relies on the Law for these will miss the peace of the Gospel.

Question 8. See the section on Congregationalism.

Question 9. See "Statements of the Episcopalian Heritage."

Question 10. "High Church," a trait of Roman Catholics, exalts the authority of bishops, the importance of ceremonies, and the power of the sacraments. "Low Church," a trait of Evangelicals, has a lower view of all these things and emphasizes Scripture and personal experience. "Broad Church" is liberal and permissive. Lutheranism has much in common with both the High Church and the Low Church.

Chapter 5

Question 1. James Arminius was the teacher whose theology was rejected by the Dutch Calvinists at the Synod of Dort. His theology has influenced many church bodies.

Question 2. Traditional Calvinists teach total depravity, unconditional predestination to salvation or damnation, limited atonement, irresistible grace, and perseverance in grace. Arminians teach freedom of the will, conditional predestination, unlimited atonement, resistibility of grace, and the possibility of falling from grace. Scripture teaches total depravity, unconditional predestination (to salvation), unlimited atonement, resistibility of grace, and the possibility of a fall from grace.

Question 3. See "Statements of the Methodist Heritage."

Question 4. See "Grace and Free Will."

Question 5. According to Wesley, the righteousness of Christ's suffering and death (as atonement for sin) is imputed to believers as their own, but the righteousness of His holy life is not. Scripture teaches that both are imputed. Human beings cannot achieve their own sinless righteousness any more than they can atone for their sins.

Question 6. See "Full Salvation." Scripture teaches that we never reach a sinless state during this lifetime.

Question 7. The Salvation Army teaches freedom of the will and perfectionism.

Question 8. Methodists recognize that God wants Baptism and the Lord's Supper to be used in the church, and they find devotional value in them. But they do not regard them as means by which God provides forgiveness of sins, life, and salvation, except that some believe in baptismal regeneration of infants. The Salvation Army, on the other hand, maintains (wrongly) that we need not continue to use these ceremonies in the church.

The Great Commission (Matt. 28:19–20), with its command to teach and baptize, deals with the permanent work of the church's servants. Jesus was speaking of such a situation continuing to the end of history, in which His presence and support would abide with His servants carrying out these tasks.

The permanence of the Lord's Supper is confirmed in 1 Cor. 11:26, "Whenever you eat this bread and drink this cup, you proclaim the Lord's death until He comes."

Question 9. The name Pentecostal indicates the claim that the apostles' experience at Pentecost is necessary for the full spiritual life of every Christian.

Question 10. See "The 'Full Gospel' of the Pentecostal Churches." Also see Col. 2:6–13.

Question 11. The Pentecostal means a special emotional experience in which the Holy Spirit starts to dwell within a person. Scripture, however, teaches that the Spirit dwells and works in all true believers from the beginning of their spiritual life (1 Cor. 3:16; 12:13).

Question 12. See Heb. 12:6–11 and 1 John 5:14; children of God may suffer according to His will. But see also 1 Thess. 1:3–4 and 2 Cor. 13:8–11; note the value of strengthened faith.

Question 14. Pentecostals teach that the ability to speak in tongues is necessary initial evidence of being baptized and filled with the Holy Spirit, that speaking in tongues spiritually transforms one's life, and that it is a more direct communion with God than a personal relationship with Him through believing His Word. Scripture does not support any of these claims.

Chapter 6

Question 1. If justification were based on Christ-in-us, this would mean that God accepted us because of the holy lives and works that the indwelling Christ empowers us to have. He does dwell in us and empower us. But we are justified solely on account of His own perfect righteousness, which is imputed to us.

Question 2. Scripture rejects pacifism—the view that God's Word never permits war. God has given the power of the sword to the government (Rom. 13:1).

Christians must not conform to the wicked attitudes and practices of the unbelieving world. But Scripture does not teach that this nonconformity must include nonuse of telephones and the like. Of course, at times self-denial in many things is necessary for faithfulness to Christ (Mark 8:35–37).

Question 3. See "The Quakers." The emphasis on the Inner Light underlies their views about the use of Scripture, the ability to cooperate with God in conversion, the "silent meeting," and unimportance of sacraments and ministers.

Christians should value the light they have from God (Eph. 5:8; 1 John 1:7). But this is not a light that they have before conversion and apart from God's Word (Eph. 5:8; 2 Cor. 4:4–6).

Question 6. (a) It is a mistake to think that heartfelt experience of Christ includes cooperation with God in bringing about one's regeneration. (b) Nor should we refuse to baptize infants on the ground that they can't have a conscious experience of life with Christ.

Question 7. Infants are part of the "nations" (Matt. 28:19). Since they are sinful at birth, they can benefit from Baptism's cleansing (John 3:6; Eph. 5:25–26). Lutherans reject the objections to infant Baptism. It is not "useless," but is a saving means of grace (1 Peter 3:21). It is not "immoral," forcing something on an infant without its consent, but is one of the most precious gifts parents can give to their children. It is not "unnecessary," but is a much-needed cleansing and regeneration.

Question 9. Scripture does not require Baptism by immersion. See "Font or River?"

Question 11. Scripture forbids drunkenness (Rom. 13:13), but not drink itself. It is included in Christian liberty (1 Tim. 4:4; Ps. 104:15). Teetotalism is taught by Baptists, Methodists, the Holiness bodies, and others.

Chapter 7

Question 1. See "Liberalism" in this chapter.

Question 2. See "Unionism" and "Union without Unity." This leads to doctrinal confusion and inability to make fully united confessions of faith. Unionism frustrates members who want to be faithful to God's truth.

Question 3. See the discussion about "Cooperative Agencies." Note problems that occur when groups exist without thorough doctrinal agreements and when the members agree to disagree in doctrine and other matters.

Question 4. The union churches include the Disciples of Christ, the Moravians, the community churches, the United Church of Canada, the United Church of Christ, and some others. We object to their method of union without unity.

Question 5. The Restorationist movement carried on by the Disciples of Christ aims to restore the principles and practices of the New Testament church. We can applaud the general aim. We can agree that no departures from New Testament teaching should be allowed. However, the New Testament does not advocate union without unity and does not allow us to tolerate false doctrine. Also, the Restorationists regard as necessary some practices that actually belong in the area of Christian liberty.

Question 6. We enjoy Christian liberty in all matters that God has neither commanded nor forbidden in His Word. But we are to be guided by love in our use of liberty; therefore we will be willing to waive our rights at times and will refrain from doing things that would hurt, confuse, or mislead our fellow Christians and neighbors (Rom. 14–15; 1 Cor. 8).

Question 7. Premillennialists teach that the Second Coming of Christ will occur before the 1,000 years of glory. Postmillennialists teach that He will return after the 1,000 years. Problems are pointed out in "General Themes" and "Millennialism." Lutherans and many others regard the 1,000 years of Rev. 20:6 as a symbol of Christ's work in His church between the Ascension and the Second Coming.

Question 8. Seventh-Day Adventists have added the ideas of the investigative judgment beginning in 1844, the completion of the atonement, qualification for eternal life by works, the Satan scapegoat, soul sleep, and annihilation. These notions disagree with what Scripture teaches about atonement, faith and works, life after death, and eternal damnation.

Question 9. See the section "Sabbatarianism."

Question 10. God does not have a different basis of salvation in different dispensations. Scripture disagrees with the Dispensationalist idea that the Gospel of grace (Acts 20:24) and the Gospel of the kingdom (Matt. 24:14) are two different messages of salvation. The lost and condemned sinner can only be saved by grace.

Chapter 8

Question 1. Unitarian-Universalists deny that there is a Trinity and that the second person of the Trinity took flesh in order to die for humanity's sins. They maintain that we can obtain salvation without a divine payment for sin. If they were right, we would lose the heart of the Gospel. See "The Unitarian Angle."

Question 2. This claim contradicts passages like Matt. 25:46. The Acts 3:21 passage refers to a restoration of *things* (relationships and conditions), not *persons*.

Question 3. They deny the Trinity, the deity of Jesus, His resurrection, His visible return, and justification by grace through faith alone.

Question 4. Such attempts contradict Matt. 24:36.

Question 5. According to the Mormons, all gods are exalted humans.

Christ, they teach, is a child born to the Father. His atoning death simply earned resurrection for sinners. Sinners themselves must earn the place they will have in eternity.

Hell is punishment that someday will come to an end.

People are justified by works, not faith alone.

Question 6. If they were not in the Mormon church, such people would be afraid their Baptism was not valid before God, that they were not in Christ's church, that they would not go to Paradise when they died, and that they could never have the benefits that are promised to those who are in a right relationship with God. If they were in the Mormon church, they would be afraid to leave it, because they would not want to take a chance on "losing" the benefits. Note the great joy and peace that are brought to us by the Gospel (and true membership in Christ's church)!

Question 7. The Worldwide Church of God does not share St. Paul's hope of enjoying a glorified body, like Christ's risen body (Phil. 3:21). The same is true of Christian Scientists, Spiritualists, Theosophists, and many New Agers, as well as what Jehovah's Witnesses say about the 144,000.

Question 8. The Science religions claim to offer the science, or knowledge, of the way to achieve health, success, and happiness. But the real knowledge that leads to happiness is Christ-centered (Eph. 1:17–22).

Question 9. Christian Science says that God is only a principle to be used, neither a personal being nor a trinity of persons. But see 2 Tim. 1:12 and Matt. 28:19.

Christ is merely the Christ idea, the truth about reality and illusion. But see 1 John 1:7.

Sin is an illusion, an imaginary problem, since every human being is God. But see 1 John 1:8.

Death is also an illusion. But see Heb. 2:14.

Question 10. Christian Science teaches that one can be healed from sickness by strongly affirming that it does not exist. But the Bible teaches that sickness is real. Christians trust in the Lord to heal it or to give strength and patience to bear it (Ps. 103:3; 2 Cor. 12:9–10). They look forward in faith to the final deliverance from it (Rev. 21:4).

Question 11. See " 'Self-evident' Propositions?"

Question 13. Spiritualism denies the personality of God, the deity of Christ, the vicarious atonement, the resurrection of the body, and eternal damnation. It seeks to communicate with the dead, which Scripture forbids.

Question 14. See "The Forerunners" in the New Age religion section.

Question 16. All these groups promise a knowledge of "truth" of which others are ignorant. They promise satisfaction by spreading the "truth," or even suffering for it. The Witnesses and Mormons offer the hope of glorious, exalted positions in the world to come, even (in the case of the Mormons) the possibility of becoming gods. Christian Science and New Age religions claim to use inexhaustible sources of power to heal and to solve problems right now in this life. They give the assurance (attractive to many) of being identical with God.

Statistics

Following are membership statistics of churches mentioned in this course. Remember that some bodies count infants as members, while others count only adults. Also, up-to-date annual reports are not available from all groups, and some churches have a large overseas constituency not included in these numbers.

Baptist

American Baptist Churches in the U.S.A.	1,396,700
National Baptist Convention of America	3,500,000
National Baptist Conventions, U.S.A., Inc.	5,000,000
Progressive National Baptist Convention, Inc.	2,500,000
Southern Baptist Convention	16,270,315

Christian Churches

Christian Church (Disciples of Christ)	722,823
Christian Churches and Churches of Christ	1,071,616
Churches of Christ	10,460

Church of the Nazarene	636,296

Eastern Orthodox

Greek Orthodox Archdiocese of North and South America	1,500,000
Orthodox Church in America	1,064,000
Romanian Orthodox Episcopate	1,500
Serbian Orthodox Church	67,000

The Episcopal Church	2,247,819

Friends

Friends United Meeting	42,680
Evangelical Friends International	27,360

Independent Fundamental Churches of America	61,655

International Council of Community Churches	108,806

Jehovah's Witnesses	1,046,006

Latter-Day Saints

Church of Jesus Christ of Latter-Day Saints	5,690,672
Reorganized Church of Jesus Christ of Latter-Day Saints (Community of Christ)	180,339

Lutheran

Evangelical Lutheran Church in American	4,850,776
The Lutheran Church—Missouri Synod	2,440,864

Mennonite

Mennonite Church	109,315
Old Order Amish Church	80,820

Methodist

African Methodist Episcopal Church	2,500,000
African Methodist Episcopal Zion Church	1,440,405
Christian Methodist Episcopal Church	850,000
The United Methodist Church	8,075,010

Moravian Church in America	23,377

Pentecostal

Assemblies of God	2,830,861
Church of God (Cleveland, Tenn)	1,013,488
The Church of God in Christ	13,822
Church of the Foursquare Gospel	326,614

Presbyterian Church (USA)	3,098,842

Reformed

Christian Reformed Church in North American	272,130
Reformed Church in America	269,815

The Roman Catholic Church	69,135,254

Salvationists

American Rescue Workers	3,500
The Salvation Army	422,543

Seventh-Day Adventist Church	964,811
Unitarian Universalist Association	214,738
United Church of Canada	1,441,000
United Church of Christ	1,224,297

Bibliography

Chapter 1

Backman, Milton V., Jr. *Christian Churches of America: Origins and Beliefs.* New York: Scribner's, 1983.

Forell, G. F. *The Protestant Faith.* Philadelphia: Fortress Press, 1960.

Häggland, Bengt. *History of Theology.* Trans. Gene Lund. St. Louis: Concordia Publishing House, 1968.

Hudson, Winthrop. *Religion in America.* 3d ed. New York: Scribner's, 1981.

Jacquet, Constant H., Jr., ed. *Yearbook of American and Canadian Churches.* Nashville: Abingdon Press (annual).

Leith, J. H., ed. *Creeds of the Churches.* Atlanta, GA: John Knox Press, 1982.

Lueker, Erwin L. *Lutheran Cyclopedia.* St. Louis: Concordia, 1975.

Mayer, F. E. *The Religious Bodies of America.* 4th ed. St. Louis: Concordia, 1961.

Mead, F. S. *Handbook of Denominations in the United States.* Rev. Samuel Hill. 9th ed. Nashville: Abingdon Press, 1990.

Piepkorn, A. C. *Profiles in Belief.* 4 vols. New York: Harper & Row, 1977–79.

Prange, Victor. *Why So Many Churches?* Milwaukee, WI: Northwestern Publishing House, 1985.

Rosten, Leo. *A Guide to the Religions of America.* St. Louis: Bethany Press, 1963.

Spitz, Lewis W. *Our Church and Others.* St. Louis: Concordia, 1969.

Chapter 2

Allbeck, Willard D. *Studies in the Lutheran Confessions.* Philadelphia: Fortress Press, 1952.

Koehler, E. W. A. *Summary of Christian Doctrine.* St. Louis: Concordia, 1952.

Kolb, Robert. *The Christian Faith. A Lutheran Exposition.* St. Louis: Concordia, 1993.

Sasse, Hermann. *Here We Stand.* New York: Harper and Bros., 1938; reprint, Adelaide, South Australia: Lutheran Publishing House, 1979.

Tappert, T. G., ed. *The Book of Concord: The Confessions of the Evangelical Lutheran Church.* Philadelphia: Fortress Press, 1959.

Wentz, Abdul Ross. *A Basic History of Lutheranism in America.* Philadelphia: Fortress Press, 1964.

Chapter 3

Flannery, Austin E, ed. *Documents of Vatican II.* Grand Rapids: Wm. B. Eerdmans, 1975.

Hardon, J. A. *Modern Catholic Dictionary.* Garden City, N. Y.: Doubleday, 1980.

Neuner, J., and Dupuis, J., eds. *The Christian Faith in the Doctrinal Documents of the Catholic Church.* New York: Alba House, 1982

Langford-James, R. L. *A Dictionary of the Eastern Orthodox Church.* New York: B. Franklin, 1975.

Mastrantonis, George. *A New-Style Catechism on the Eastern Orthodox Faith for Adults.* St. Louis: Ologos, 1969.

Chapter 4

Clark, Gordon. *What Do Presbyterians Believe?* Phillipsburg, N.J.: Presbyterian & Reformed Publishing, 1956.

Holmes, Urban T. *What Is Anglicanism?* Wilton, Conn.: Morehouse-Barlow, 1982.

Lingle, Walter, and John W. Kuykendall. *Presbyterians: Their History and Beliefs.* Atlanta: John Knox Press, 1978.

McNeill, John T. *The History and Character of Calvinism.* New York: Oxford University Press, 1954.

Osterhaven, M. Eugene. *The Spirit of the Reformed Tradition.* Grand Rapids: Wm. B. Eerdmans, 1971.

Chapter 5

Bloch-Hoell, N. E. *The Pentecostal Movement.* New York: Humanities Press, 1964.

Harmon, Nolan. *Understanding the United Methodist Church.* Rev. ed. Nashville: Abingdon Press, 1977.

Hollenweger, Walter. *The Pentecostals.* Minneapolis: Augsburg Publishing House, 1972.

McKinley. E. H. *Marching to Glory* [History of the Salvation Army in the USA.] New York: Harper, 1980.

Chapter 6

Cole, E. B. *The Baptist Heritage.* Elgin, IL: David C. Cook Publishing Co., 1976.

Hobbs, Herschel H. *What Baptists Believe.* Nashville: Broadman Press, 1964.

Trueblood, D. Elton. *The People Called Quakers.* New York: Harper & Row, 1966.

Wenger, J. C. *What Mennonites Believe.* Scottsdale, PA: Herald Press, 1977.

Chapter 7

Commission on Theology and Church Relations of The Lutheran Church—Missouri Synod. *The End Times.* St. Louis: Concordia, 1989.

——. *A Lutheran Stance Toward Ecumenism.* St. Louis: Concordia, 1974.

——. *The Nature and Implications of the Concept of Fellowship.* St. Louis: Concordia, 1981.

Clouse, R. *The Meaning of the Millennium: Four Views.* Downer's Grove, IL: Intervarsity Press, 1977.

Gerstner, John H. *A Primer on Dispensationalism.* Phillipsburg, N. J.: Presbyterian & Reformed, 1982.

Hedegard, David. *Ecumenism and the Bible.* Rev. ed. London, WI: Banner of Truth Trust, 1964.

Horton, Douglas. *The United Church of Christ.* New York: Thomas Nelson, 1962.

Hoekstra, H. T. *Evangelism in Eclipse.* World Mission and the World Council of Churches. Greenwood, SC: Attic Press, 1979.

Jackson, Gregory. *Liberalism: Its Cause and Cure.* Milwaukee: Northwestern, 1991.

Martin, Walter. *The Truth about Seventh-Day Adventism.* Grand Rapids: Zondervan, 1960.

Rouse, R., S. C. Neill, and Harold E. Fey, eds. *A History of the Ecumenical Movement.* 2 vols. London: SCM Press, 1967–70.

Seventh-Day Adventists Believe . . . Washington, D.C.: Ministerial Association. Conference of Seventh-Day Adventists, 1988.

Teegarden, K. L. *We Call Ourselves Disciples.* St. Louis: Bethany Press, 1976.

Williams, D. D., and R. L. Shinn. *We Believe: An Interpretation of the United Church Statement of Faith.* New York: United Church Press, 1966.

Chapter 8

Ball, John M. *Saints of Another God. Mormon History, Culture, and Religion.* Milwaukee: Northwestern Publishing House, 1989.

Hoekema, Anthony. *Christian Science.* Grand Rapids: Wm. B. Eerdmans, 1974.

How to Respond Series. St. Louis: Concordia. (Booklets on how to respond to various cults.)

Larson, Bob. *Bob Larson's Book of Cults.* Rev. ed. Wheaton, IL: Tyndale House, 1989.

——. *Straight Answers on the New Age.* Nashville: Thomas Nelson, 1989.

Martin, Walter. *The Kingdom of the Cults.* Minneapolis: Bethany House Publishers, 1985.

Martin, Walter, and Norman Klann. *Jehovah of the Watchtower.* Minneapolis: Bethany House, 1981.

Tucker, Ruth. *Another Gospel. Alternative Religions and the New Age Movement.* Grand Rapids: Zondervan, 1989.

Winker, Eldon K. *The New Age Is Lying to You.* St. Louis: Concordia, 1994.